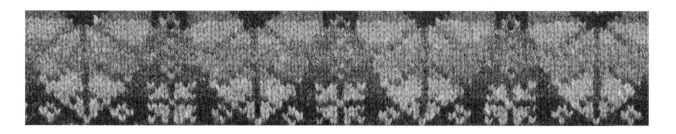

Alice Starmore's

Charts For Color Knitting

New and Expanded Edition

D1296335

DOVER PUBLICATIONS, INC.
Mineola, New York

Bibliographical Note

This Dover edition, first published in 2011, is a new and expanded edition of *Charts For Colour Knitting*, orginally published by The Windfall Press, Scotland, in 1992.

International Standard Book Number

ISBN-13: 978-0-486-48463-1
ISBN-10: 0-486-48463-7

Manufactured in the United States by Courier Corporation
48463703
www.doverpublications.com

Contents

Introduction

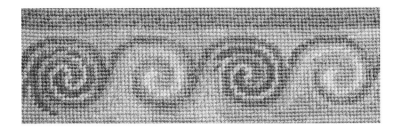

As a professional designer, my pattern library is my single, most valuable resource—as important as a broad palette of coloured yarn. It might seem strange that a collection of dots upon a page is so vital, but pattern is the very first element I turn to when designing a garment. It is a framework which affects all that follows. The pattern controls how I use colour, and gives an underlying coherence to my colour scheme. In the sphere of traditional knitting, it is a large body of patterns—used boldly and consistently—that confers regional or national identity.

This book contains a comprehensive selection from my pattern library; some collected, some adapted from various forms of artwork, and some from my own imagination. In the chapters that follow, I hope to share my own fascination with dots upon a page, and show that they have a similar power to words. Someone without even a grain of mathematical ability can still possess a well-developed geometric sense, and can gain pleasure from a pattern, just as if it were a well-turned phrase in a novel or poem. Different patterns have different effects. Those mundane dots can excite, intrigue or elevate, and they can even tease. A complex, interlacing allover might be found to be the result of a small, innocuous repeating unit. Above all, I hope to convey a spirit of adventure and excitement at the design potential that pattern offers, for despite the vast hoard of patterns already produced, there are still an infinite number waiting to be discovered. The limits are only set by our imaginations.

Designing Patterned Sweaters

Designing a colour-patterned sweater can be much easier than its complex beauty suggests, and my aim is to provide you with a clear guide to the process involved. I find it is best to explain by example, and so I invite you to "look over my shoulder" as I design a small collection of sweaters which will serve as a guide for applying patterns to your own designs. I have used a simple, dropped shoulder pullover shape which is the easiest to begin with but the points covered here will also serve as a basis for designs with more complex shapes.

This book contains four different types of charted patterns—single motifs, allovers, horizontal borders and vertical panels. Similarly, the collection contains four sweaters, each based on one of these types of pattern. In this way I will cover all the points you need to know when using the patterns for your own personal garments.

I always begin with a theme which will give the collection a unifying identity. For this exercise, I have chosen *Autumn*, which immediately conjures up specific images such as harvest, leaves, berries, fruits, and a rich association of colours. This provides me with a focus, and I then look at my pattern library for anything which will evoke these images.

At this stage I also think about other references that will give me ideas for adapting or designing new patterns. Autumn leaves for example, or anything else from the natural world. This is one of the ways in which I build up my source material. Having decided on the patterns to use, I then draw rough sketches of the designs, as shown here. I would like to emphasise that you do not have to be a great artist to do this. The main point is to see what you are planning.

Once I have sketched the designs, I think about yarns. Quality and colour are my most important considerations, as without the very best, the finished result will invariably be a disappointment. The weight of yarn also affects the size of the pattern when knitted—thick yarn will make the pattern larger, thin yarn will make it smaller. For example, in the single motif design I would like the motifs to appear fairly large and bold on the sweater, so I will use **Alice Starmore**® *Hebridean 3 Ply* yarn for the main body. The allover, border and panel designs are smaller in scale, so I will use **Alice Starmore**® *Hebridean 2 Ply*.

The next step is to knit a swatch for each design. There are three vital reasons for doing so. First, I can see how the patterns look when knitted up, and make any necessary changes. Second, I can judge the effectiveness of my colour scheme. Third, I use my swatch to determine the number of stitches and rows to any given measurement—in other words, my tension. This is necessary in order to convert the design into accurate working instructions.

The swatch should always be large enough for the pattern and colour scheme to be clearly viewed, and for an accurate tension measurement to be made. I always make my swatch at least 10cm (4in) width and length for a lightweight yarn, and at least 15cm (6in) for a heavier yarn. Bearing this minimum in mind, my swatches will vary in size depending on the size and combination of patterns that I plan to use. I will discuss this further when I deal with each design in turn. As you work through this chapter, use either metric or inch measurements, but do not combine the two.

Single Motif Sweater

This is an ideal starting point for knitters who have never designed sweaters before. Single motifs can be worked on a basic stocking stitch sweater to produce an endless variety of original and beautiful results. A plain sweater with just one motif carefully placed is easy to knit and yet can make a bold statement.

For this sweater I have used a variety of different motifs I designed from my *Birds & Flowers* collection on Pages 124 and 125, and scattered them over the design virtually at random.

Generally, it is best to knit the single motif patterns using the intarsia method. This involves using separate lengths or balls of yarn for each different colour in each motif,

rather than carrying the yarns from one motif to the next. This avoids the need to carry the motif yarns over long distances. The alternative method is to knit the sweater entirely in the background yarn and swiss darn (duplicate stitch) the motifs in later. Sometimes a combination of both is the best option. For example, you could intarsia-knit the motif in the dominant colour, then swiss darn the small touches of colour on completion, as I have done on the swatch shown on page 6.

If you want to avoid calculating the instructions for knitting the sweater, you may use an existing design and place your chosen motifs in any way you please. Either use the written instructions for a basic sweater design which suits you and graph out all the stitches, rows and shapings in the manner shown in the chart opposite, or use an existing charted design and rechart the outlines. You can then place your motifs on the chart. If you do this you must use the same weight of yarn as the original design and make sure that your tension is exactly the same as that given for the original, otherwise the sweater will not turn out to be the size specified. For example, you may use the chart opposite and replace the motifs with your own choice, but you will need to use the same weight of yarn and work at the same tension as I have stated in order to produce the given size.

Making the swatch

You **must** knit a swatch—whether you use an existing pattern or work out your own instructions. For a design with single motifs, I make my swatch large enough to work a complete motif with roughly 3cm (1in) of plain background all around it. For this design, I will knit one of the larger motifs and gain a really good idea of how the design will look.

Right: Chart for single motif sweater

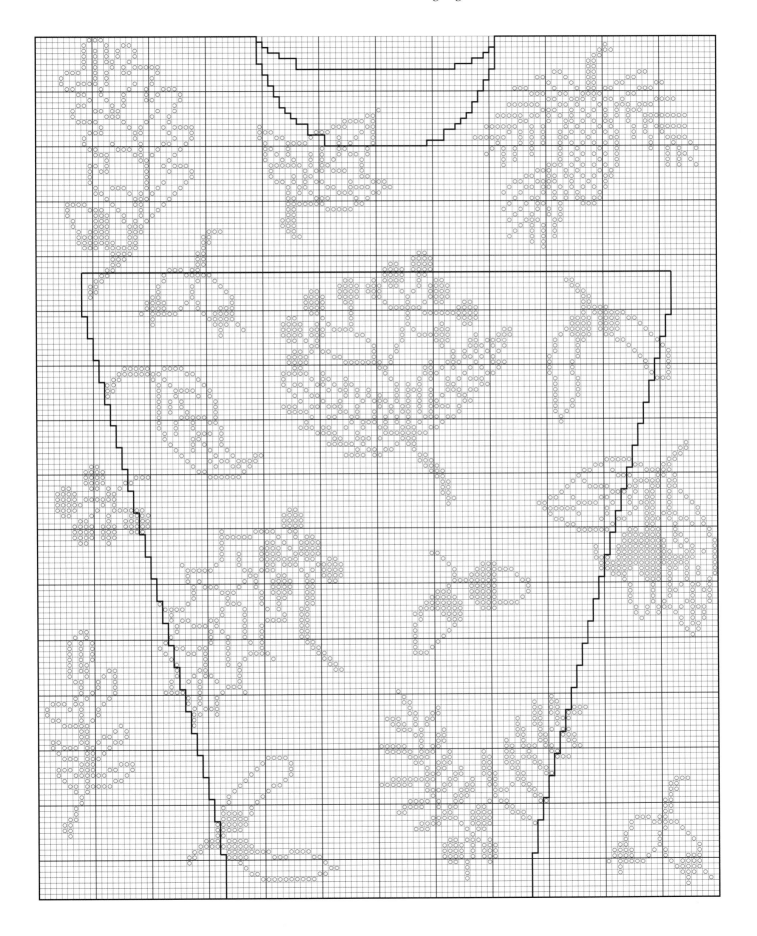

Drawing the measurement plan and calculating the knitting instructions

The main advantage in calculating your own instructions is that you have freedom to work with any type of yarn, and you can produce any size and shape of sweater. Here is how I calculated the chart for this design. First I drew the measurement plan shown here, and I plotted all the required measurements for a simple shape. My tension was 22 sts and 28 rows to 10cm using **Alice Starmore**® *Hebridean 3 Ply* and 4.5mm (US 7) needles. Using my tension, I converted the necessary measurements into the required number of stitches and rows, as shown opposite.

A	54.5cm	(21.5in)
B	56cm	(22in)
C	7.5cm	(3in)
D	23.6cm	(9.25in)
E	32.4cm	(12.75in)
F	17.7cm	(7in)
G	19cm	(7.5in)
H	7cm	(2.8in)
I	8cm	(3.25in)
J	2cm	(0.75in)
K	12.75cm	(5in)
L	40.75cm	(16in)
M	6.5cm	(2.5in)
N	47.25cm	(18.5in)
O	24.5cm	(9.7in)

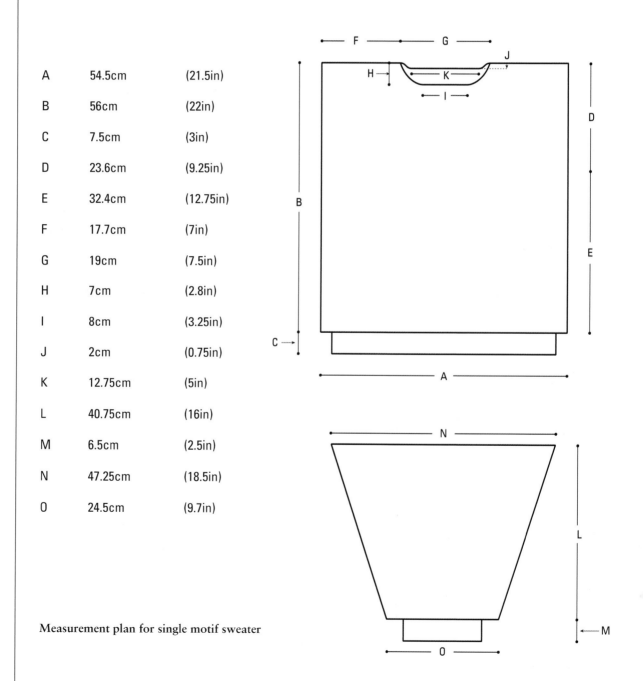

Measurement plan for single motif sweater

If 10cm = 22 sts and 28 rows then:

A 54.5cm (21.5in) = 120 sts.

B 56cm (22in) = 157 rows.

C It is not necessary to calculate the number of rows for the rib. I will simply knit to the desired measurement. To make the rib tighter I will use smaller sized needles. If I want a closer fitting rib, I will cast on fewer sts (roughly 10% fewer than **A**) and increase to **A** on the last row of rib.

D & E Again, it is not necessary to convert these measurements for this design as there is no armhole shaping. Instead, I will place a marker at the armhole position when I reach measurement **E**.

F 17.7cm (7in) = 39 sts.

G 19cm (7.5in) = 42 sts.

H 7cm (2.8in) = 19.6 rows. Half rows cannot be worked, so I will take this result to the next largest number: i.e. 20.

I 8cm (3.25in) = 18 sts. I can now calculate the number of sts to be decreased at each side of the front neck by subtracting **I** from **G**: i.e. 42 - 18 = 24.

This leaves 12 sts to be decreased at each side, which must be decreased within the 20 rows of **H**. In order to give the neckline a rounded shape, I will cast off 3, then 2, then decrease 1 at the edge of the next three rows, and decrease 1 at the edge of the next 4 alternate rows. The remaining 6 rows will be worked straight.

Note: The shaping on the right neck edge (see the charted outline on page 9) begins 1 row further up because a purl row has to be worked before the shaping can begin. This is why the neckline is 1 row higher on this side.

J 2cm (0.75in) = 6 rows. This measurement is converted into the next largest number of rows.

K 12.75cm (5in) = 28 sts. I can now calculate the number of sts to be decreased at each side of the back neckline by subtracting **K** from **G**: i.e. 42 - 28 = 14 sts.

This leaves 7 sts to be decreased at each side, which must be decreased within the 6 rows of **J**. To shape, I will cast off 3, then 2, then decrease 1 at the edge of the next 2 rows. The remaining 2 rows will be worked straight. The shaping on the left neck edge begins 1 row further up, for the same reason as with the front neck.

L 40.75cm (16in) = 114 rows.

M Treat as **C**; knit the rib on smaller needles and approx 25% fewer sts than **O** for a close fit. I will increase to the full number on the last row of rib.

N 47.25cm (18.5in) = 104 sts.

O 24.5cm (9.7in) = 54 sts. I can now calculate how many sts I need to increase at each side of the sleeve, by subtracting **O** from **N**: i.e. 104 - 54 = 50.

This gives 25 sts to be increased at each side, which should be increased as evenly as possible within the 114 rows of **L**. To calculate, divide as follows—
114 rows divided by 25 increases = 4 with remainder 14.

I want the sleeve to be slimmer just above the cuff so I have placed the first pair of increases after working 8 rows, and the next pair on the following 6th row and thereafter on every following 4th row. Then finally working 7 rows straight at the top.

I can now chart out all my calculations to produce the charted outline shown on page 9. With that completed, I can chart in the motifs, and the design is ready to be knitted.

Allover Sweater

J ust as its name suggests, the allover pattern is worked continuously both horizontally and vertically. In this design, it is worked in classic fashion over the entire sweater. I designed this small allover based on the idea of a leaf and a kernel. The sweater shape is the same as the first design, but the measurements are for a slimmer fit.

As the pattern is continuous horizontally, it is highly suitable for stranded knitting—working each row with two colours, a background and a pattern, and stranding the yarn not in immediate use across the back of the work. The entire design can be worked in just two colours, or the colours can be changed row-by-row in any way you

please. I would strongly recommend knitting all stranded patterns in circular fashion, and working steeks at all openings. This method is faster, easier, and produces a better finish than working flat pieces. This is because the pattern is worked in knit stitches on the right side, with the pattern always facing. Seams are also eliminated, and where knitted steeks are worked, darning-in ends is avoided. For a complete guide on designing and knitting circular sweaters with steeks, see *Alice Starmore's Book of Fair Isle Knitting* (Dover Publications, Inc., 2010).

Making the swatch

Having established that I will knit the design in circular fashion, I need to knit my swatch accordingly. As I will not be working purl rows in the sweater, I do not want to work them in the swatch, as this would alter my tension (knit and purl rows have a slightly different tension). To simulate circular knitting I knit the swatch on either two double-pointed needles, or a circular needle, working on the right side only and breaking off the yarns at the end of every row. To avoid loose stitches at each end I give the yarn ends a good tug as I go along. To make the swatch I will work two horizontal repeats of the pattern (see **Chart 2** on page 14), casting on 40 stitches and working 40 rows. This will be enough to give a good view of the pattern and to measure the tension accurately.

My tension is 28 stitches and 32 rows to 10cm, using **Alice Starmore**® *Hebridean 2 Ply* and 3.25mm needles.

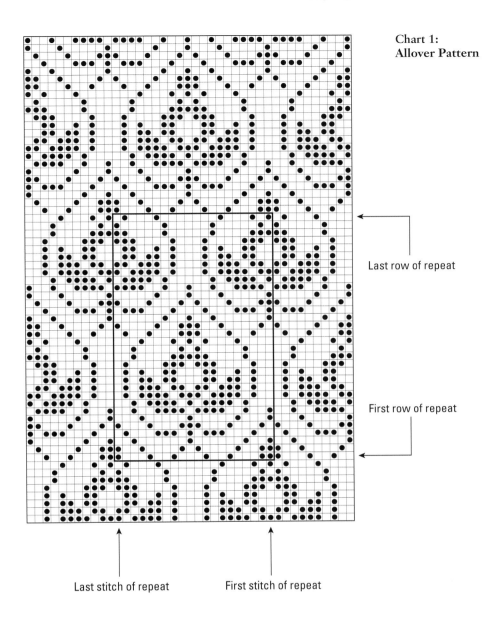

Chart 1:
Allover Pattern

←── Last row of repeat

←── First row of repeat

Last stitch of repeat   First stitch of repeat

Finding the pattern repeat and charting the pattern

The allover pattern consists of motifs which repeat both horizontally and vertically. It is important to establish the number of stitches and rows in a single repeat in order to fit the pattern exactly into the design. To do this I begin with the horizontal stitches, and start the repeat at a centre stitch in the pattern—in this case the stitch which runs between the first row of complete motifs and through the centre of the next row of motifs, as indicated on **Chart 1** above. This centre stitch is the first stitch in the repeat. Moving leftward, I count the stitches until I reach the same centre stitch again. The repeat finishes immediately before the next centre stitch, and contains twenty stitches.

It makes sense to start the row repeat at the centre of a motif in a pattern of this type, and it would be perfectly correct to do this. However, as the motifs are not symmetrical on either side of the centre row, I find that the pattern is aesthetically more pleasing when it begins on the row I have marked, and so I will make this the first row of the repeat. Moving upwards, I then count the rows until I reach the first row again. The repeat finishes immediately before this row and contains 32 rows.

I can now chart out a single repeat as shown in **Chart 2** below. The rows are numbered at the right side of the chart because every row begins on the right when working in the round.

Chart 2

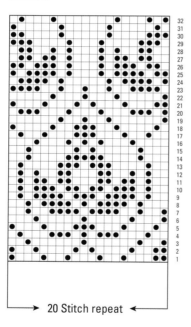

→ 20 Stitch repeat ←

Generally, if the pattern is symmetrical about a centre row, it is best to begin at the centre. Otherwise any position which looks good is acceptable. I have designed allovers with a definite starting edge, worked only once at the start, and with the row repeat beginning above it. A good example is my Celtic pattern on page 87, where the row repeat begins at the centre of the first large diamond.

Drawing the measurement plan and calculating the knitting instructions

For a circular sweater I draw the measurement plan shown opposite. Using my tension measurement, I can now convert the measurements into stitches and rows in the same way as for the first design. I will assume that you are now familiar with the process, and will only discuss the particular points which apply to working with the allover pattern on the circular sweater.

Fitting patterns around the body

The pattern repeat should divide exactly into **A**, the all-round width of the sweater. I require 280 sts for the 100cm (39.25in) width. The 20 st repeat divides into 280 sts exactly 14 times, which means that the pattern will repeat exactly 14 times around the sweater. Of course, the result is often not so convenient, in which case some adjustment will have to be made. The total number of stitches may be adjusted if the count is out by a very small amount. However this does alter the measurement and there is a limit to this solution. To keep as close to the desired width as possible, it may be necessary to change the size of the stitch repeat.

For example, if **A** was 120cm (47.25in), I would require 336 sts. The 20 st repeat clearly will not divide exactly. However, a 24 st repeat will divide exactly 14 times, and so I will alter the pattern to produce a 24 st repeat, as shown in **Chart 3** opposite. To alter the repeat, I marked 24 sts on graph paper and charted the motifs 4 sts further apart than in the original. I then added a couple of small motifs and extended the "branches" at the base of the motifs over 1 more row, to fill in the gaps.

Measurement plan for allover, border and panel sweaters

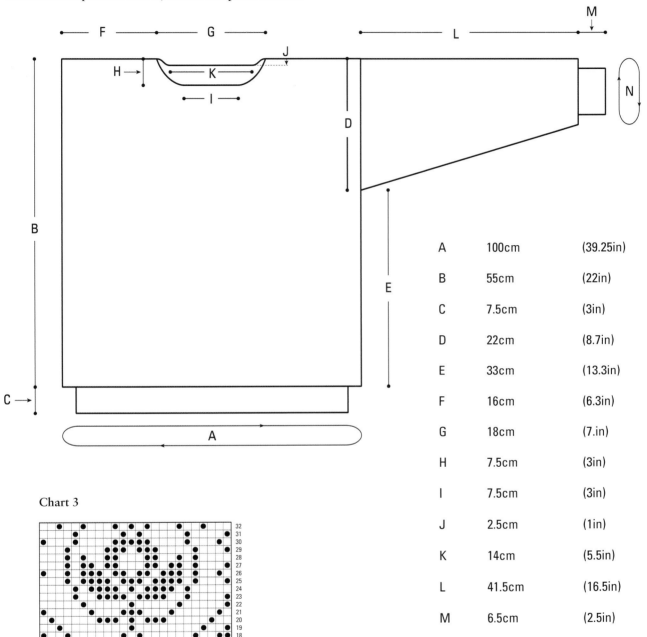

A	100cm	(39.25in)
B	55cm	(22in)
C	7.5cm	(3in)
D	22cm	(8.7in)
E	33cm	(13.3in)
F	16cm	(6.3in)
G	18cm	(7.in)
H	7.5cm	(3in)
I	7.5cm	(3in)
J	2.5cm	(1in)
K	14cm	(5.5in)
L	41.5cm	(16.5in)
M	6.5cm	(2.5in)
N	23.5cm	(9.25in)

Chart 3

24 Stitch repeat

The first and centre stitches of the round are the centre underarm stitches, which "divide" the back and front as shown below. These stitches are commonly referred to as seam stitches, although there is no seam. It is very important to centre the pattern at the back and front, for otherwise the sweater will look decidedly off-balance. If the pattern repeats into the round an even number of times and the stitch repeat begins at a centre point as I have described and charted, then the pattern will be automatically centred at the back and front, and no further calculation is necessary. However, if the pattern repeats into the round an odd number of times, then the starting point of the pattern must be adjusted at the beginning of the round, in order for it to be centred. To achieve this begin the round with the last quarter of the stitch repeat.

Fitting the patterns into the body length

Once I have calculated the number of pattern rows required in the length (measurement **B**), I check where the pattern will finish at the shoulder, so that it will meet at an appropriate row. I have 176 rows of pattern to the shoulder. To find the finishing row I divide this number by the row repeat, as follows—

176 divided by 32 gives me a result of 5 pattern row repeats plus 16 rows. This is an appropriate point at which to finish the pattern. If it were not, I would slightly alter either the length of the rib, or the total length. The shoulders are grafted together, using the colour which dominates in the next row of the chart.

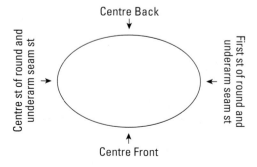

Position of underarm seam stitches

Fitting the patterns around the sleeve

To calculate how many stitches to pick up around the armhole, I multiply measurement **D** by two and then convert this measurement into stitches. In this case, I will need to pick up 123 sts. I will also pick up the body seam stitch. This stitch will not be considered as part of the pattern, but will be worked in background colours throughout, and become the sleeve seam stitch and the first stitch of the round. The decreases which shape the sleeve will be worked at either side of this stitch. To centre the pattern on the sleeve, I divide the pattern stitches picked up by the stitch repeat, which gives 6 repeats plus 3 sts. With the chart upside down, (it can be read the right way up if the pattern is symmetrical) I will begin the round with the underarm seam st which I will knit in the background colours throughout, then knit the last 2 sts of the repeat, then repeat the pattern 6 times, then knit the first st of the repeat. Once the pattern is centred, the continuity should be maintained throughout all the decrease shaping. In other words, the pattern will be "cut away" at each side of the underarm seam stitch as the sts are decreased but it will always stay centred, as shown in the photograph opposite, where the centre stitch of the allover tree pattern runs directly down the length of the sleeve, from the shoulder line. Note that the border patterns around the cuff are also centred in the same way.

Fitting the patterns into the sleeve length

I would like the pattern to finish above the cuff with the first row of the chart, as on the body. To establish on which row to start, I divide the total number of rows in measurement **L** by the row repeat.

In this case, 132 divided by 32 = 4 repeats with a remainder of 4. Therefore, to finish on the first row of the chart—working upside down—I will knit rows 4 back through row 1, then repeat the pattern from row 32 through row 1, 4 times.

To shape the sleeve, subtract the stitches in measurement **N** from the total stitches at the begining of the sleeve, and decrease the resulting stitches in pairs, placed as regularly as possible within the total patterned rows.

Oregon Autumn: showing how the allover pattern is centred on the sleeve

Horizontal Border Sweater

T his design features an arrangement of horizontal border patterns I designed for my *Birds & Flowers* collection from Pages 116 and 117. The style, size, tension and working methods are exactly as for the allover sweater, and I will only cover the new points which are concerned with this type of pattern arrangement.

Finding the pattern repeats and charting the pattern

I check the stitch repeat of each pattern while making my choice, as each pattern must repeat exactly into the all-round width of the sweater. This does not mean that each repeat need be the same. However, two of my chosen patterns have a 20 st repeat and the third has a repeat of 10 sts. This means that I can chart out the whole arrangement within 20 sts and consider it as one pattern for the purpose of fitting. I will begin charting the repeat at the centre stitch between the motifs of the larger patterns. The smaller leaf pattern has no centre stitch and so it can begin anywhere.

Before charting the arrangement, I want to be sure that the pattern finishes at an appropriate place at the shoulder, and therefore I will need to work out exactly where to begin. To do this, I first count up how many rows are in the arrangement. I will have a plain background row at the beginning and end of the two larger patterns, making these 27 and 19 rows, and I will be working the 10 row leaf pattern twice, making the total count 66 rows. I now need to see how this fits into the 176 rows of measurement **B**. This involves playing around with the numbers until the options become clear. I will go through each possibility by way of illustration.

Options

1. If I work 10/27/10/19 repeated, I will have two complete repeats plus the first 44 rows worked again. This means I will finish on the 7th row of a 10 row leaf. If I add another 3 rows to the total, I will finish on the 10th and final row of the leaf, which means that the shoulder can be grafted with the background colour, producing a leaf pattern on either side of a centre row—as shown in **Plan 1** opposite. Adding 3 rows will mean adding just under 1cm (0.4in) in length, which would be acceptable. I would consider this a good option.

2. If I work 10/19/10/27 repeated, I will finish on the 5th row of the 27 row pattern, which would be incomplete at the shoulder.

3. If I work 19/10/27/10 repeated, I will finish on the 15th row of the 27 row pattern, which would also be incomplete at the shoulder.

4. If I work 27/10/19/10 repeated, I will finish on the 7th row of the 19 row pattern. If I add 2 rows to the total, I will finish on the 9th row and can graft the shoulders together with the 10th background colour. This 10th row is the centre row of a symmetrical pattern, and if I swiss darn the pattern colour after grafting, the pattern will be continuous over the shoulder as shown in **Plan 2** opposite. This is also a good option.

Plan 1: Pattern arrangement for Option 1

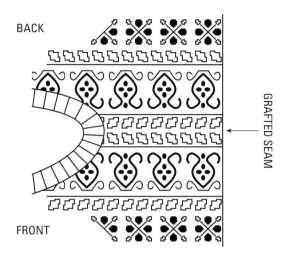

Plan 2: Pattern arrangement for Option 4

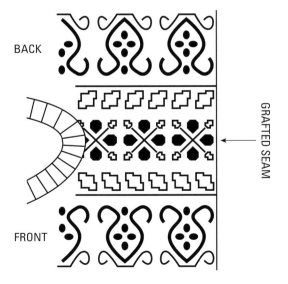

The choice is between options 1 and 4. Either will work very well, though I prefer 4 for its continuity. I can now chart out the arrangement, beginning with the 27 row pattern, as shown here in **Chart 4**.

To make the swatch, I will cast on 40 sts and work 2 stitch repeats and all 66 rows of the chart. I could work fewer rows for a tension swatch but the purpose of the swatch is also to determine how the colour scheme works and for that reason I need to see how the whole repeat will look.

The options for fitting the patterns into the sleeve length are dealt with in the same manner. If you are concerned about matching the sleeve and the body patterns so that they more-or-less line up horizontally when the sweater is worn, you should proceed as follows—

Begin the sleeve arrangement on the same row as on the body, at the beginning of the armhole, and follow the body arrangement downwards. Then continue until the sleeve is the required length. For this design, I prefer to fit in an exact number of patterns as shown here. The pattern is centred on the sleeve as described for the allover sweater.

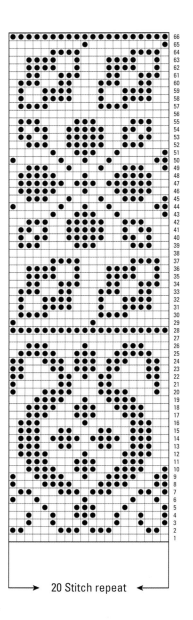

← 20 Stitch repeat →

Chart 4: Chart for knitting border sweater

Pattern arrangement on sleeve:
10/27/10/19/10/27/10/19 = 132 rows

Right: *Marina*, one of my most popular colour designs. Arrangements of border patterns are a wonderful and versatile way to express design ideas. For example, *Marina* is based on an underwater theme and worked into a classic cardigan shape. I also carried one of the patterns into the textured borders, which unifies the whole design.

Panel Sweater

T his design combines a single motif that I created for my *Birds & Flowers* patterns on page 123, an adapted vertical Norwegian vine panel from page 40 and my allover pattern from page 119. The single motif, bordered by the Norwegian vine, is worked as a vertical panel at the centre of the front, back, and sleeves. The remaining space is filled with the small allover pattern which adds interest and keeps the strands short when carrying the yarn between panels. Style, size, tension and working methods are the same as for the previous two designs, and I will only cover the points which are new to this particular design.

To make the swatch, I will work a full single motif, one Norwegian vine, and roughly 5cm of the small allover pattern.

Charting and fitting the patterns

Each pattern must be charted separately because the row repeats are different in each one. The large single motif is to be worked as a vertical panel, and I have added an extra row so that the top of the first motif will not merge into the bottom of the next. At the same time, I want to give some continuity and also avoid a long stretch in one colour. I have therefore joined the pattern at the small motifs on the 34th row, as shown in **Chart 5**. To separate each pattern vertically, I need at least 1 stitch in background between each one. I have included these stitches at each side of the Norwegian vine chart. See **Chart 6**.

Before charting the allover pattern, I need to calculate the number of stitches it will be worked over, between the back and front panels. One panel—a single motif plus the vine at each side—totals 67 sts. There are 280 sts in the sweater body. The back and front panels will account for 134 of these, leaving a total of 146 sts. Half of this total (73 sts) will be worked in the allover pattern between each panel. The allover has a stitch repeat of 8, which means that the pattern will repeat 9 times with 1 stitch extra, into each group of 73 sts. The extra stitch is essential, as the allover patterned area should start and finish with the same centre stitch at each side of the panels. I can now chart the allover pattern, with the extra stitch as shown in **Chart 7**. The round will begin at the first seam stitch which is at the centre of the allover patterned area; therefore I will set the pattern by knitting the rounds thus —

Begin at the centre of allover chart and work the last 4 sts of the repeat, then repeat the 8 pattern sts 4 times; work the last st of allover; *17 sts of vine; 33 sts of single motif; 17 sts of vine; **repeat the 8 patt sts of allover 9 times; work the last st of allover; repeat from * to ** once more; repeat the 8 pattern sts of the allover 4 times; then pattern the first 4 sts of the repeat, thus completing the round.

Next, I check where the panel will finish at the front and back neck. Because the neck necessarily cuts into the body space, it does not matter too much where the pattern finishes: it will look quite natural almost anywhere. However, I always try to avoid having the beginning of a large motif

Chart 5: Chart for single motif

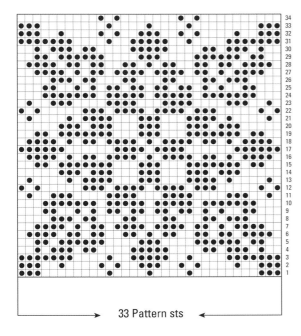

33 Pattern sts

Chart 6: Chart for Norwegian vine panel

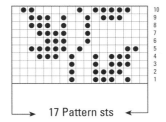

17 Pattern sts

Chart 7: Chart for small allover pattern

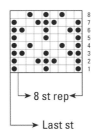

8 st rep

Last st

disappear at the neckline, and sometimes minor adjustments in the length can give a better finishing point. There are 176 rows in measurement **B**. There are 8 rows in measurement **J**. Therefore there are 168 patterned rows to the back neckline. This is just 2 rows short of exactly 5 single motifs. There are 24 rows in measurement **H** and therefore there are 152 patterned rows to the front neckline. This will be enough for 4 complete single motifs plus the first 16 rows. If I add 2 rows to the total, then I will have 5 complete motifs on the back, and will include the centre row of the 5th motif at the front. In this case, it is worth adding the 2 rows to finish at these positions. I am not concerned where the pattern finishes at the shoulder, as the allover pattern is small and asymmetric.

It is important to centre the pattern on the sleeve so that the centre stitch of the single motif is in line with the grafted shoulder seam. By adding 4 rows to the 132 rows of the sleeve, I will fit exactly 4 single motifs and add 1cm (0.5in) to the length. If necessary, the cuff rib can be shortened to compensate. The allover and vine pattern chart will be worked upside down, but this is not necessary with the single motif chart, as the pattern is symmetrical.

The centre panel, bordered with the Norwegian vine, worked in Alice Starmore® _Hebridean 2 Ply_

Traditional Knitting Patterns

The most comprehensive range of traditional knitting patterns comes from Northern Europe—more particularly, the countries surrounding the Baltic Sea, which I have referred to in previous books as the "Baltic Circle." The patterns of these countries show certain similarities, being based upon simple geometric shapes, but they have otherwise developed in quite different directions. Norway has an enormous body of patterns—the largest by far—kept within tight geometric parameters, but still extremely varied. It is a logical style, easy to knit and perfectly suited to the techniques of stranded knitting. The only diversions from the regular, geometric path, take the form of pictorial representations of people and reindeer.

Practicality is not such a strong characteristic of Swedish patterns, being somewhat more free in form, and although stylised, not so tied to regular geometric constraints. Technique was not such a vital factor in their development, and designs were often worked to capture the effects of luxury woven textiles like French brocade. Consequently they can be difficult to knit, with long stretches in one colour. The effect can be well worth the extra effort.

Across on the other side of the Baltic we have not so much a national style as a series of overlapping regions. Finland—consistent with its position at the very hub of the Baltic Circle—is a veritable melting pot of pattern styles, with small, regular geometric patterns, Swedish-style patterns, naturalistic motifs, and a sprinkling of the stepped, jagged emblems so typical of Estonia, Latvia and Lithuania. These latter countries are the most problematic, in that it is often not possible to tie a pattern to one particular nation. Hence, the three are grouped together for the purposes of this book. The geometry of the Russian patterns is also closely related to them.

The patterns from South America are all Andean in origin, and some of their elements are similar to those of Europe, contributing evidence for the concept of a basic geometric sense which transcends oceans and language barriers. In addition, South America has the marvellous range of totemic birds and animals.

One obvious omission in this section, are the patterns of Fair Isle in Scotland. My collection of Fair Isle patterns has already been published, and I would rather use this space to bring other deserving patterns into wider circulation.

Right: An arrangement of traditional Norwegian patterns knitted in Alice Starmore® *Hebridean 3 Ply* in Selkie and Pebble Beach

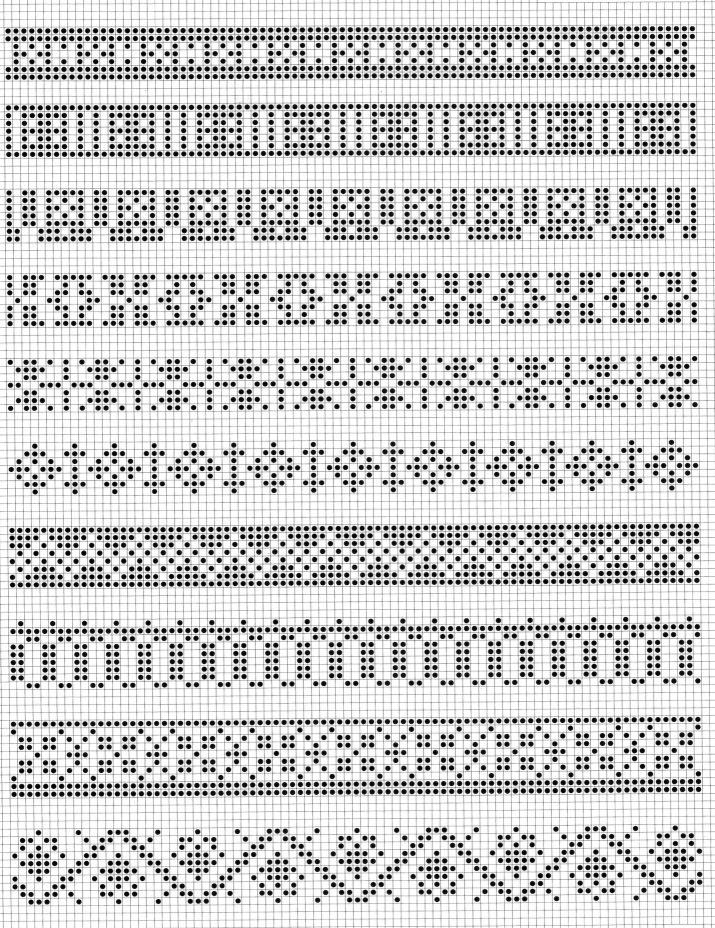

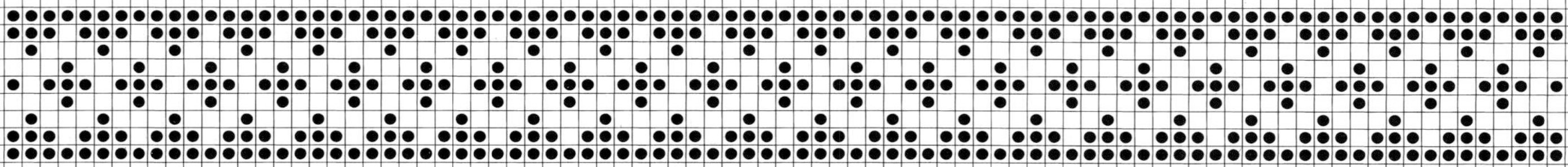

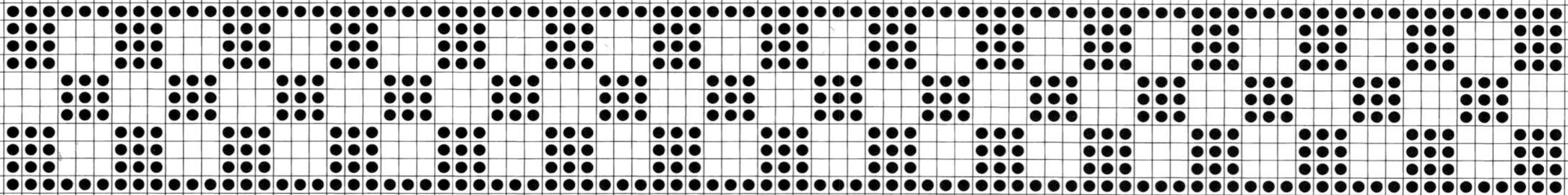

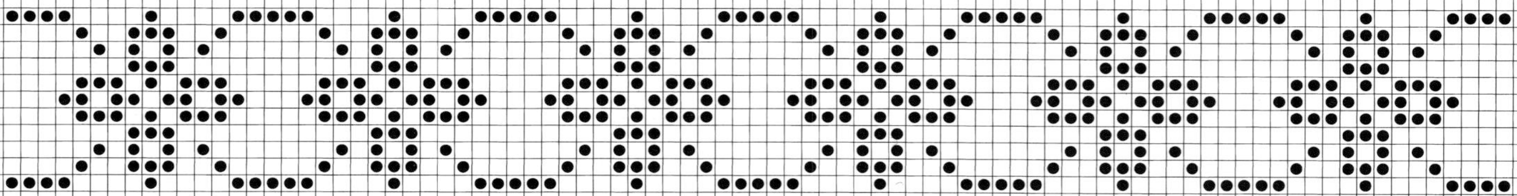

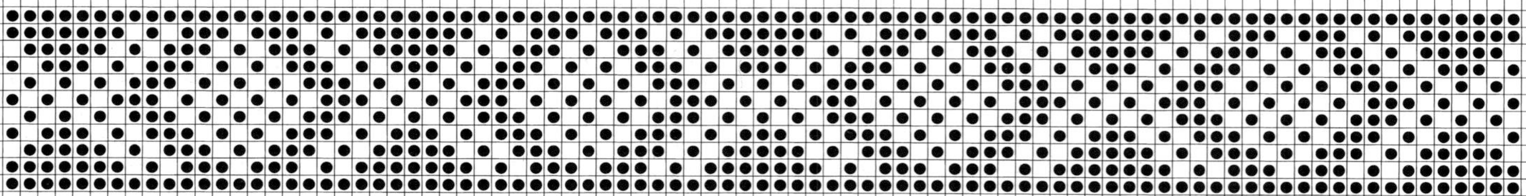

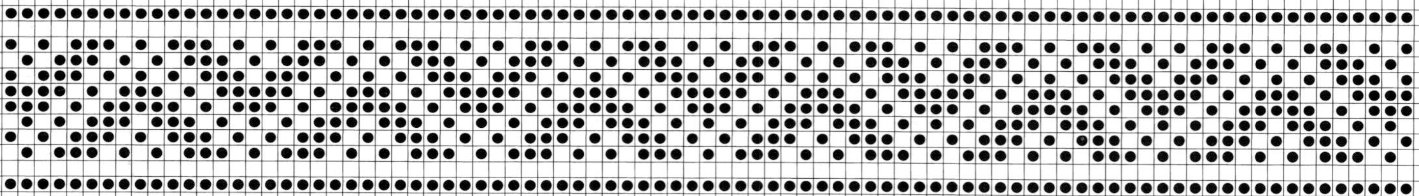

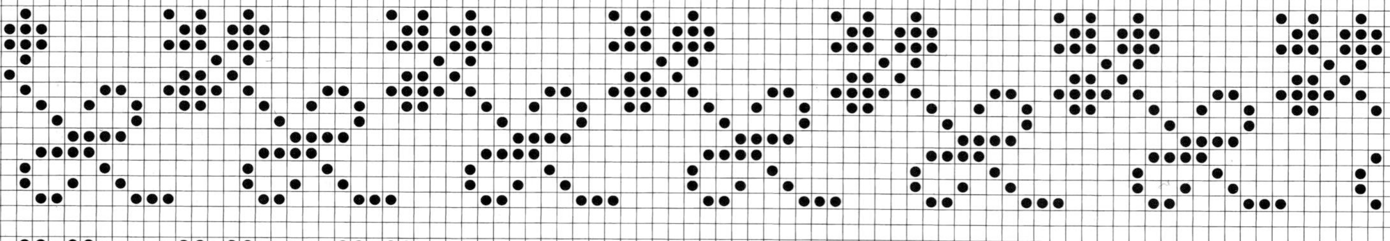

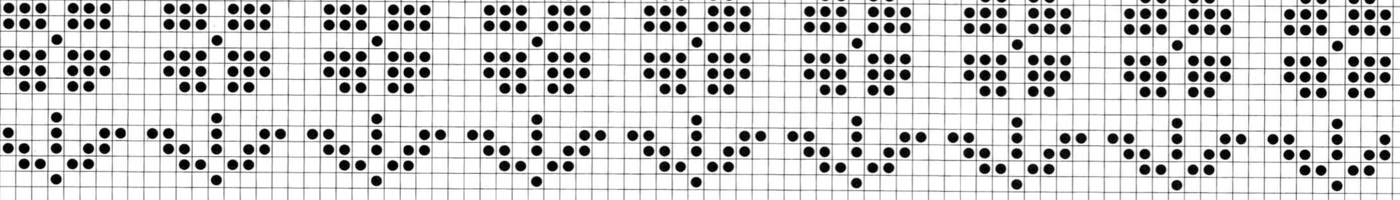

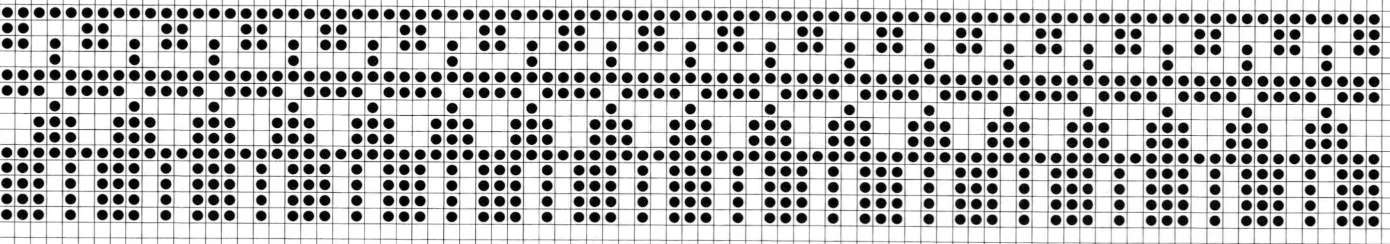

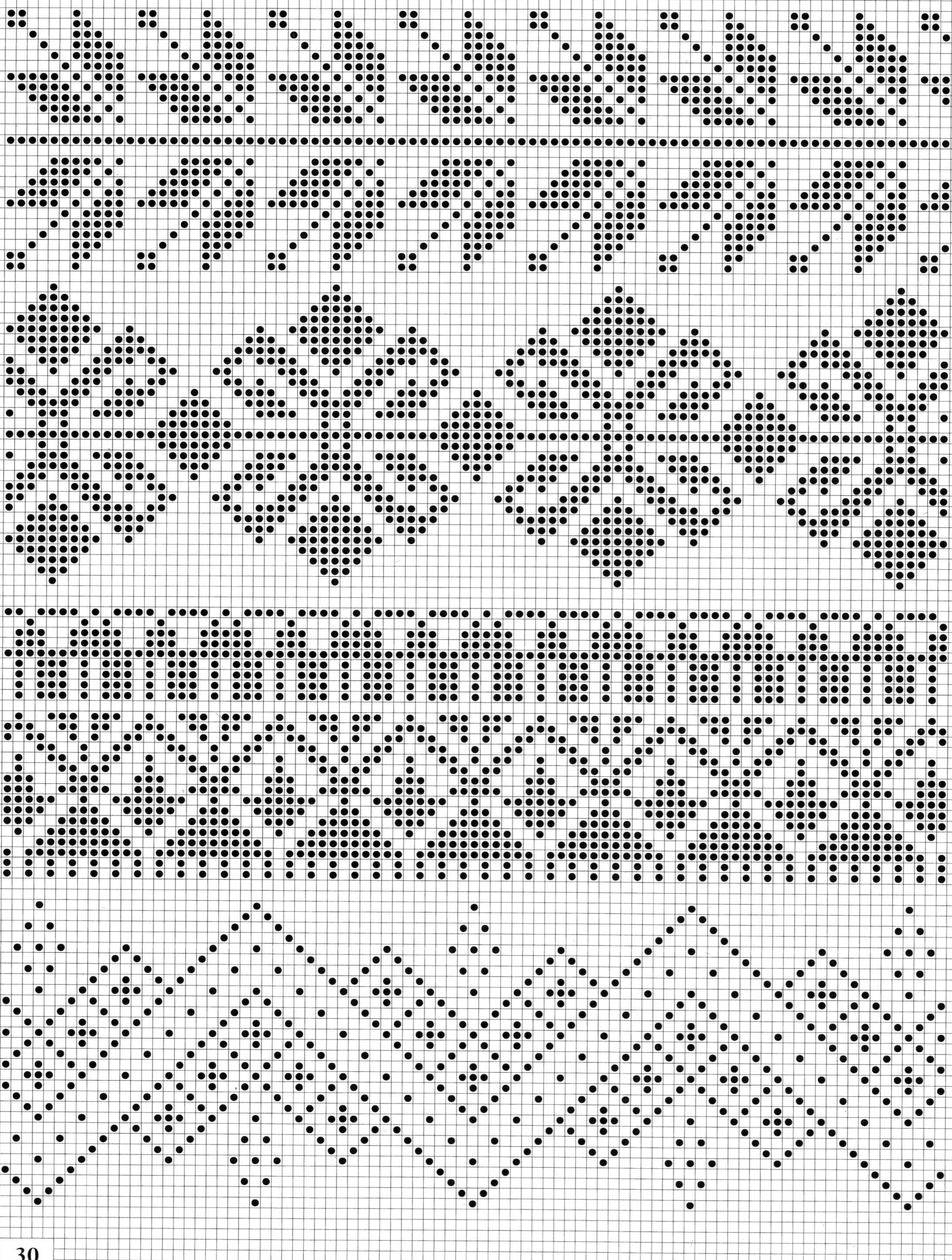

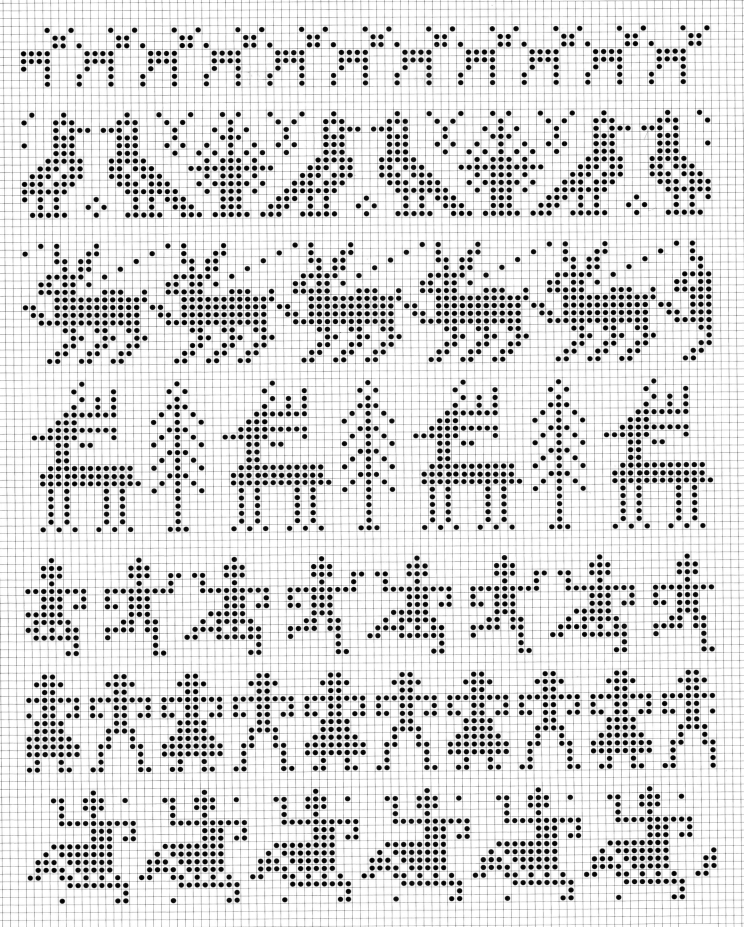

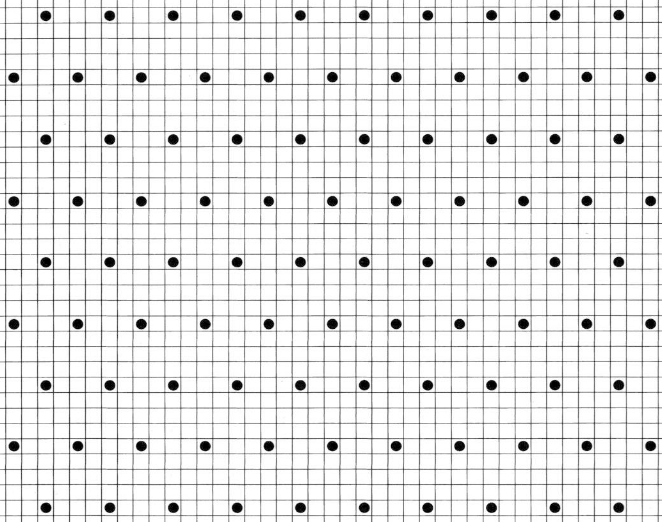

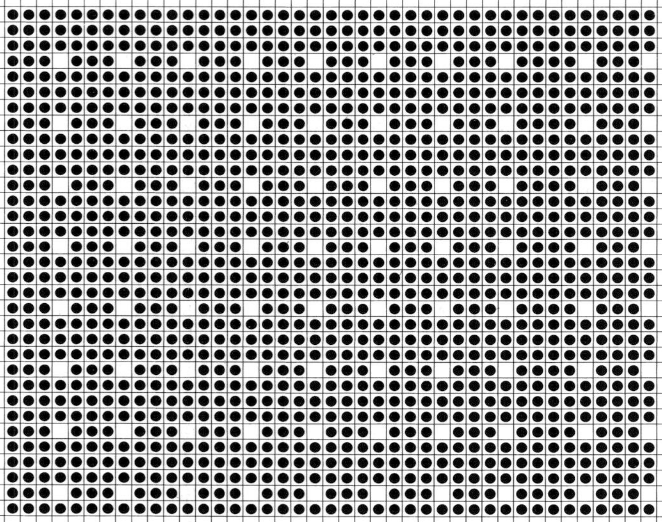

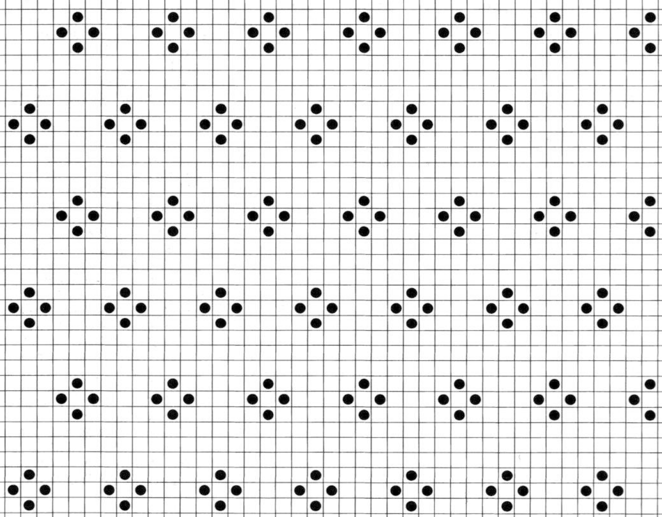

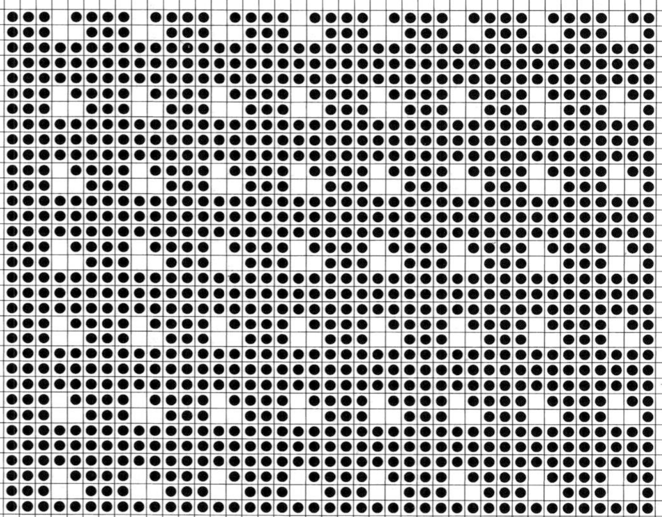

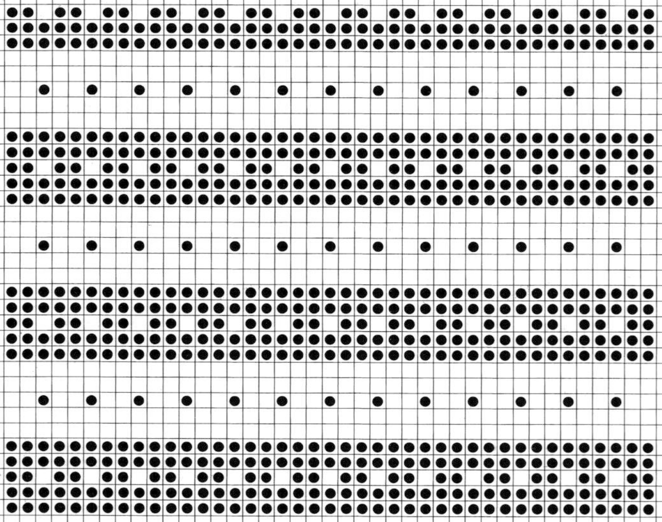

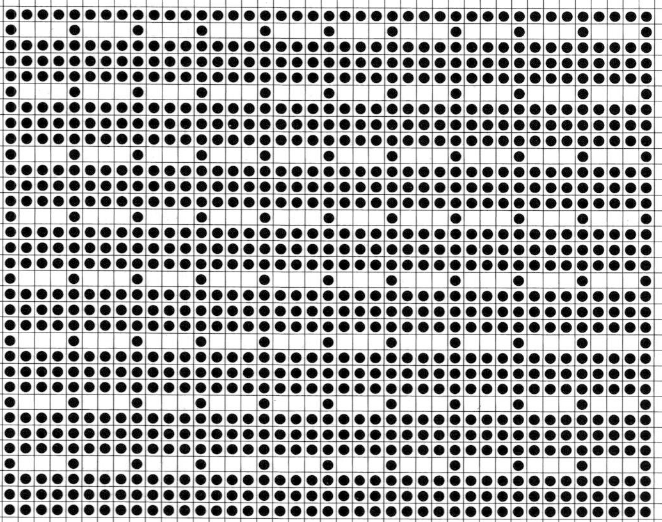

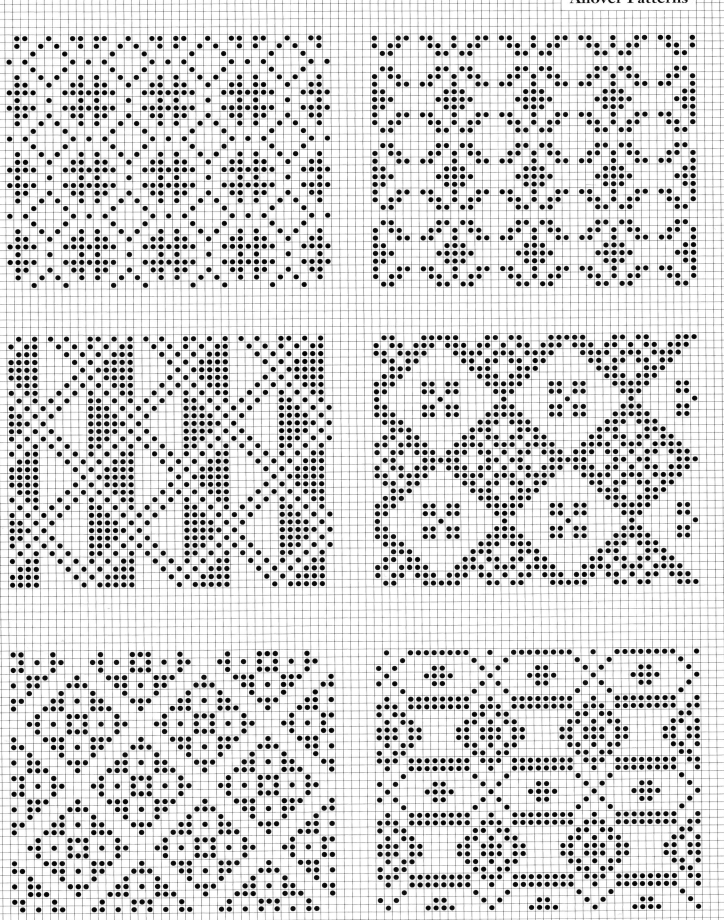

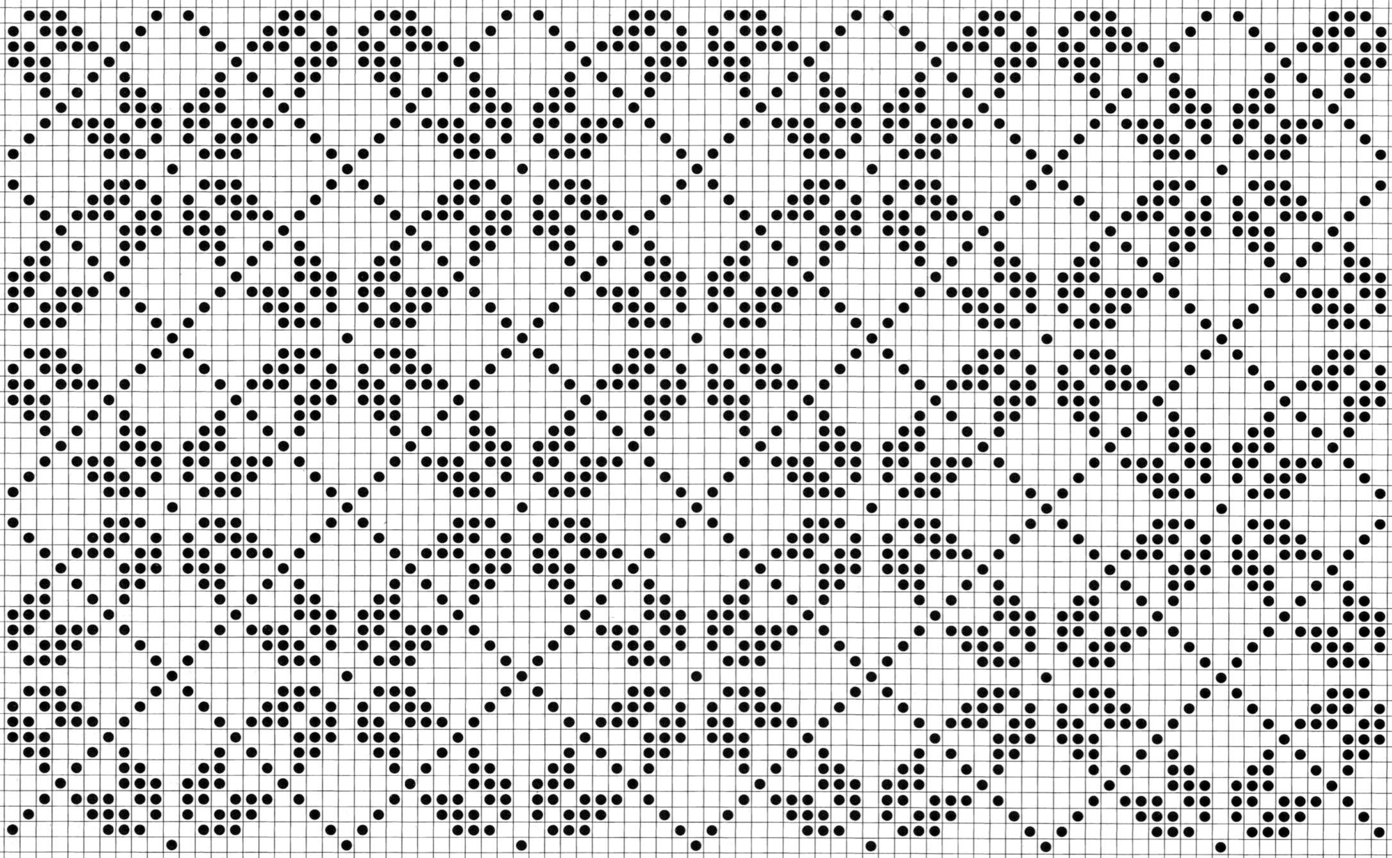

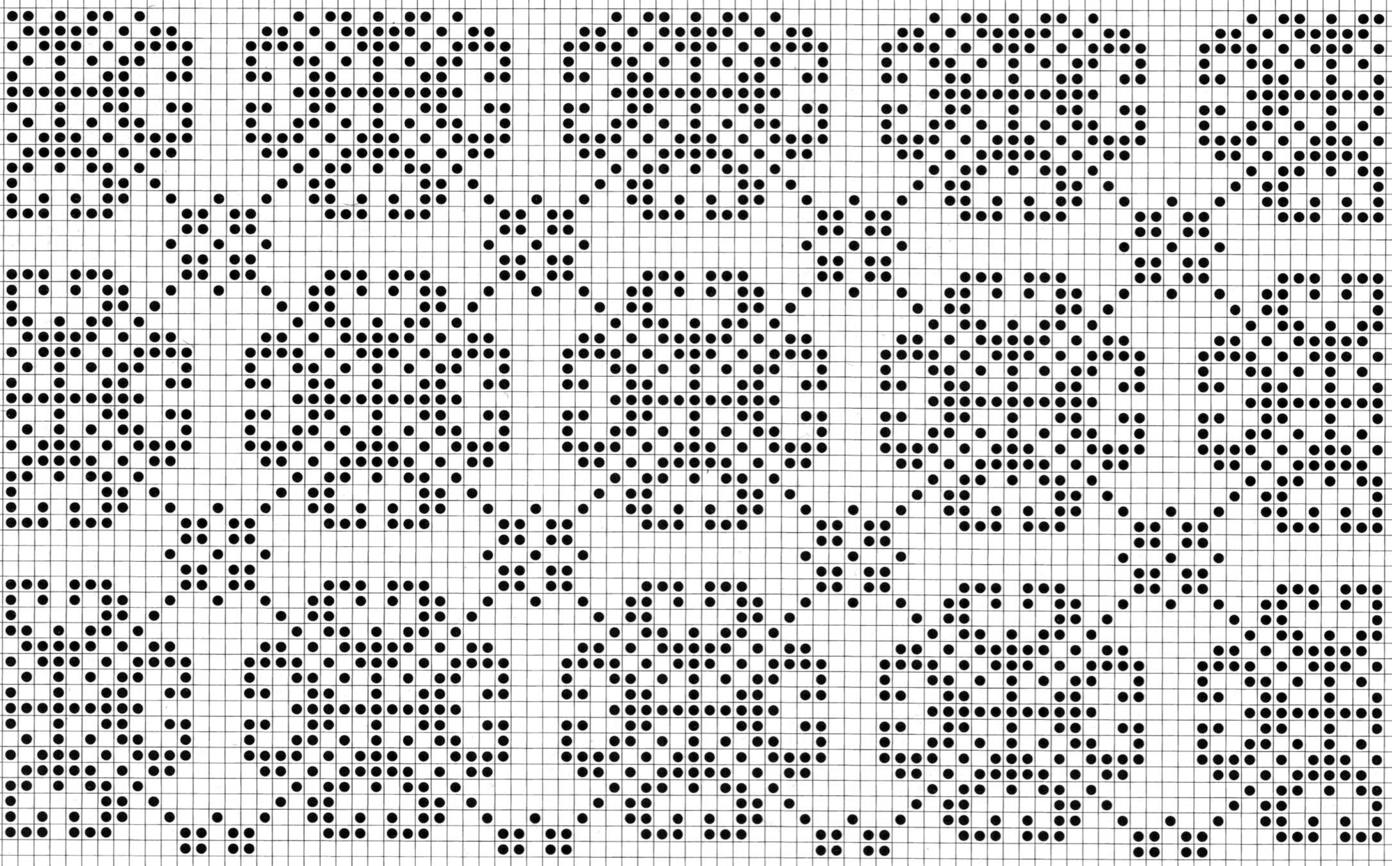

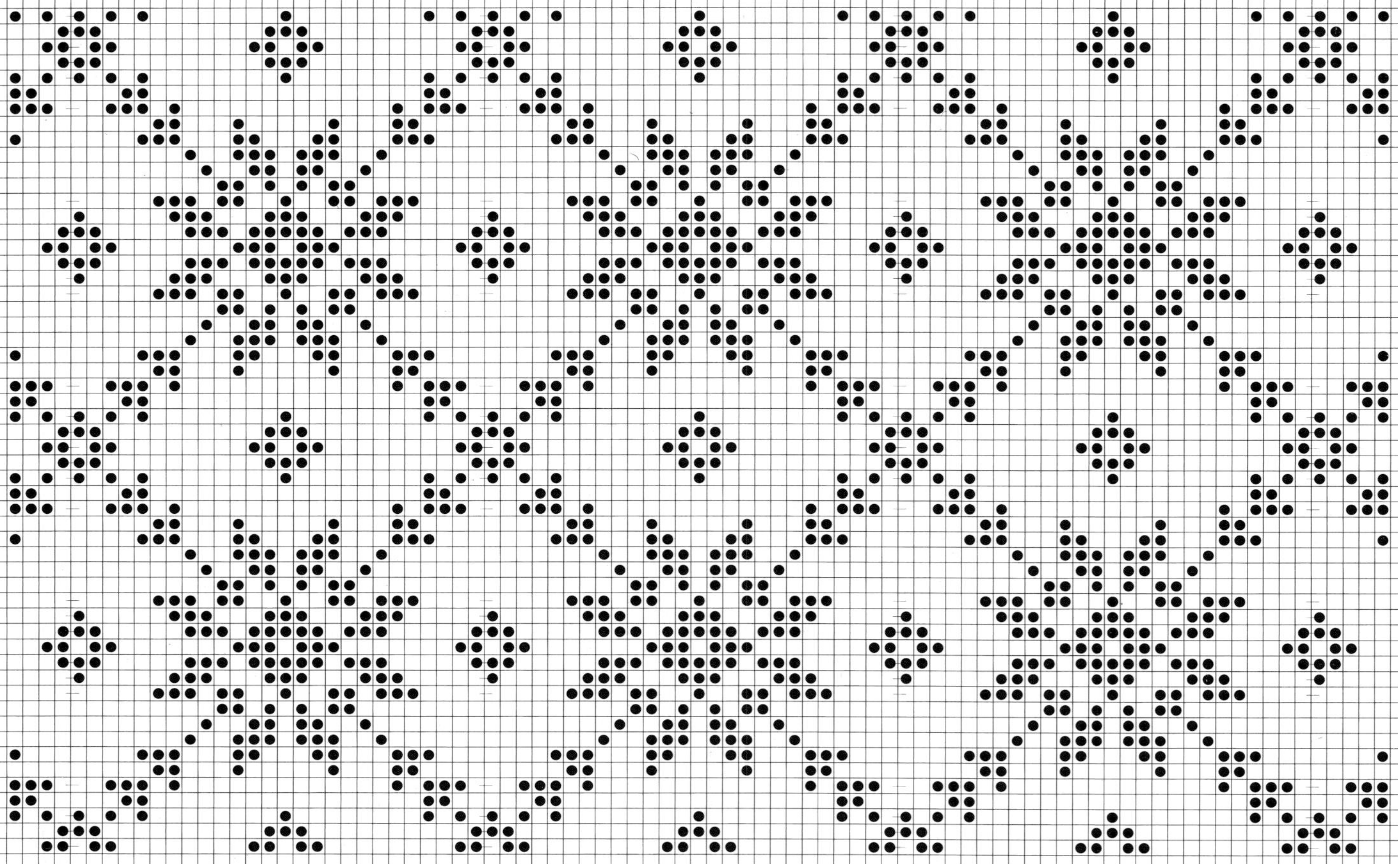

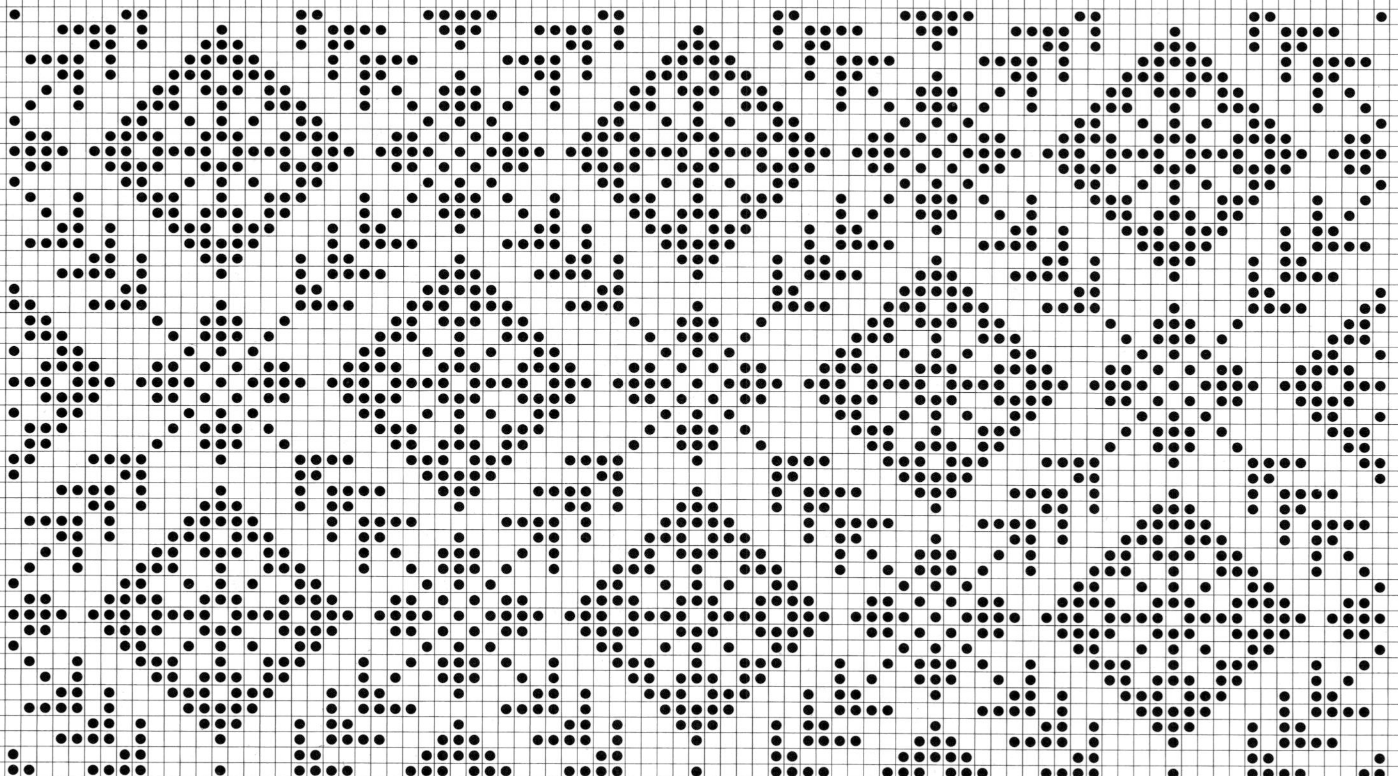

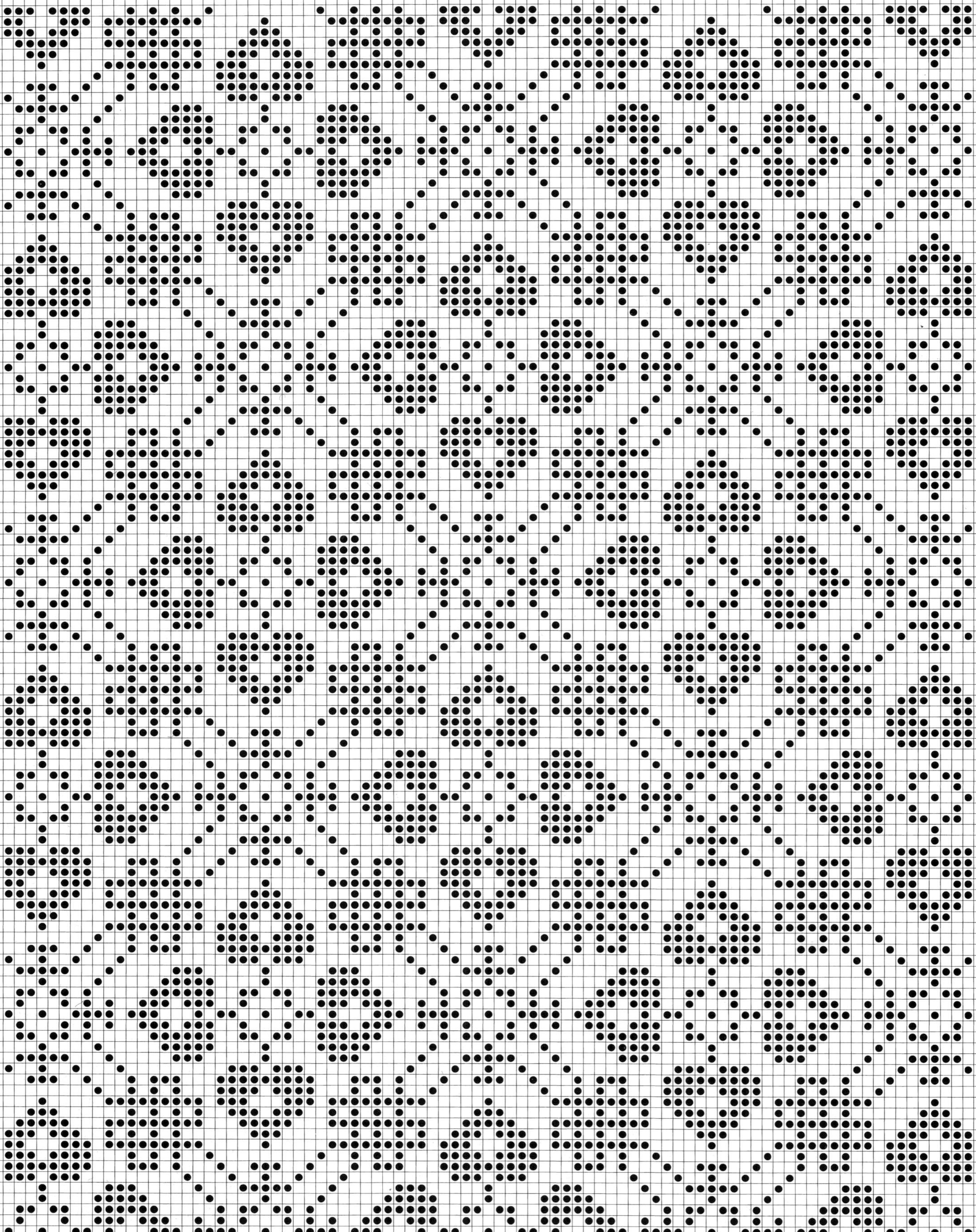

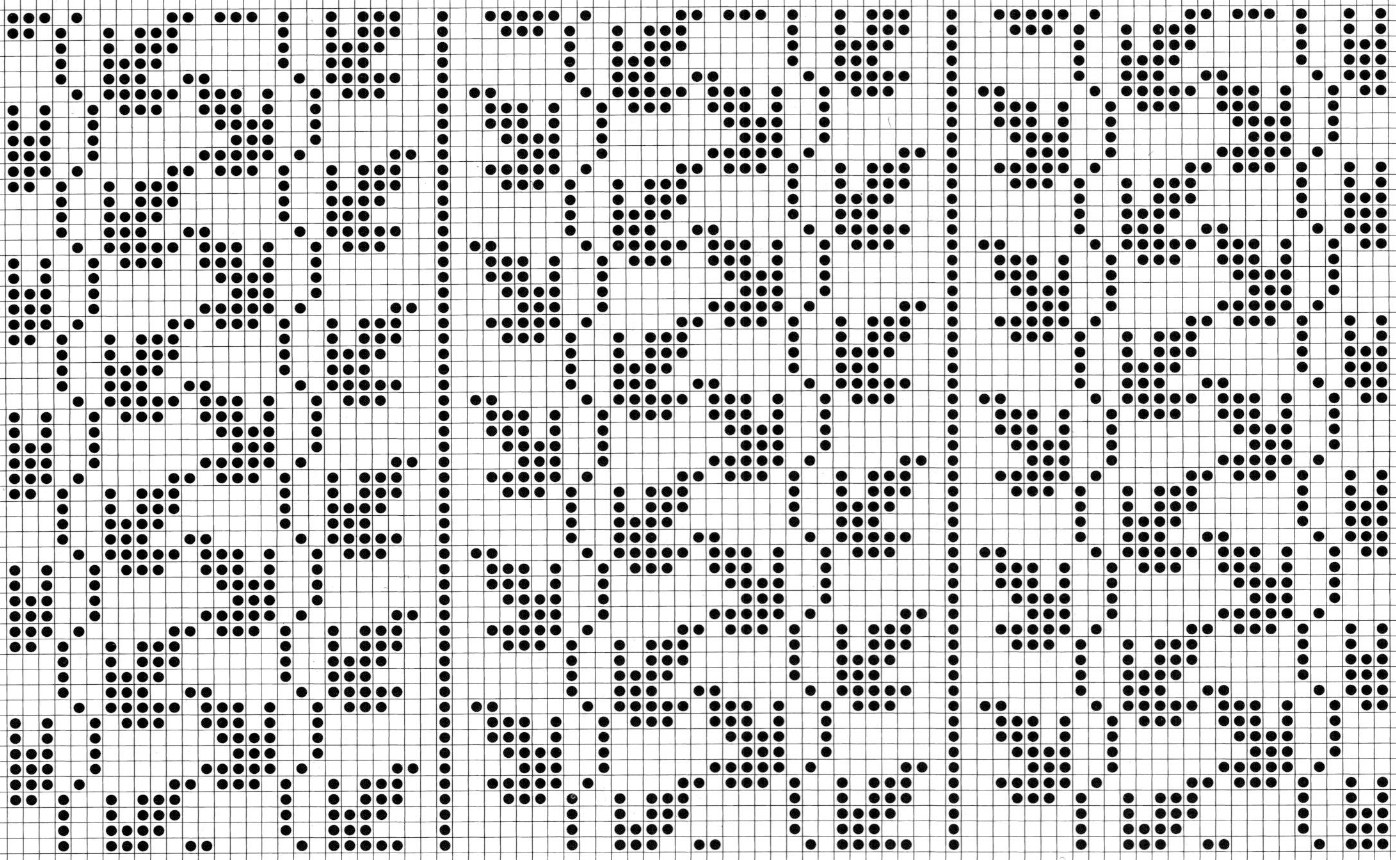

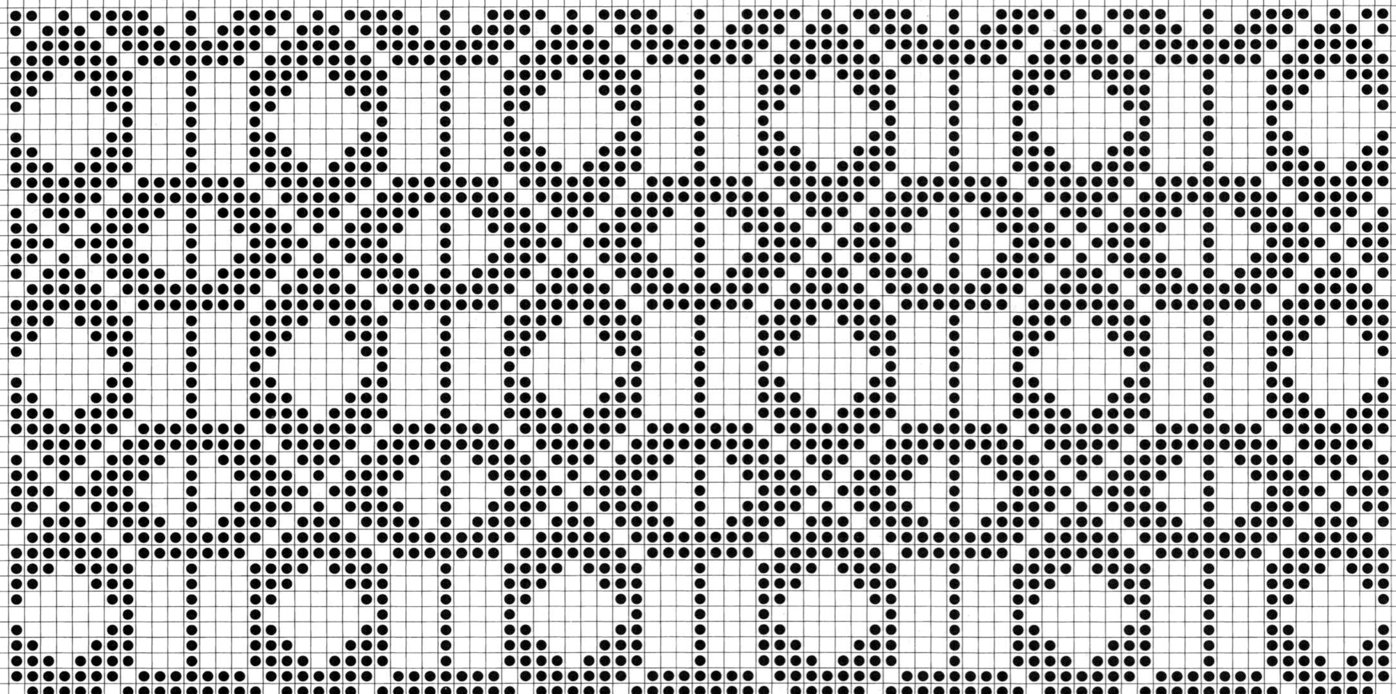

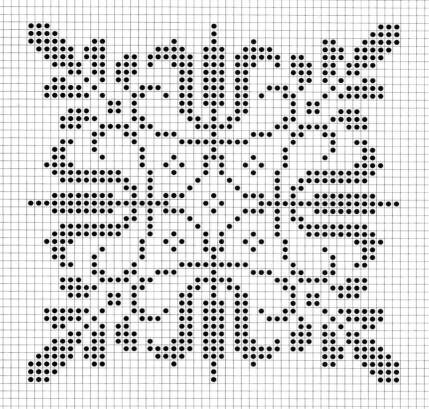

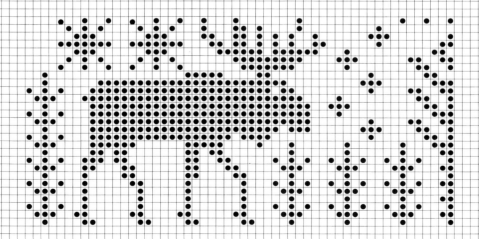

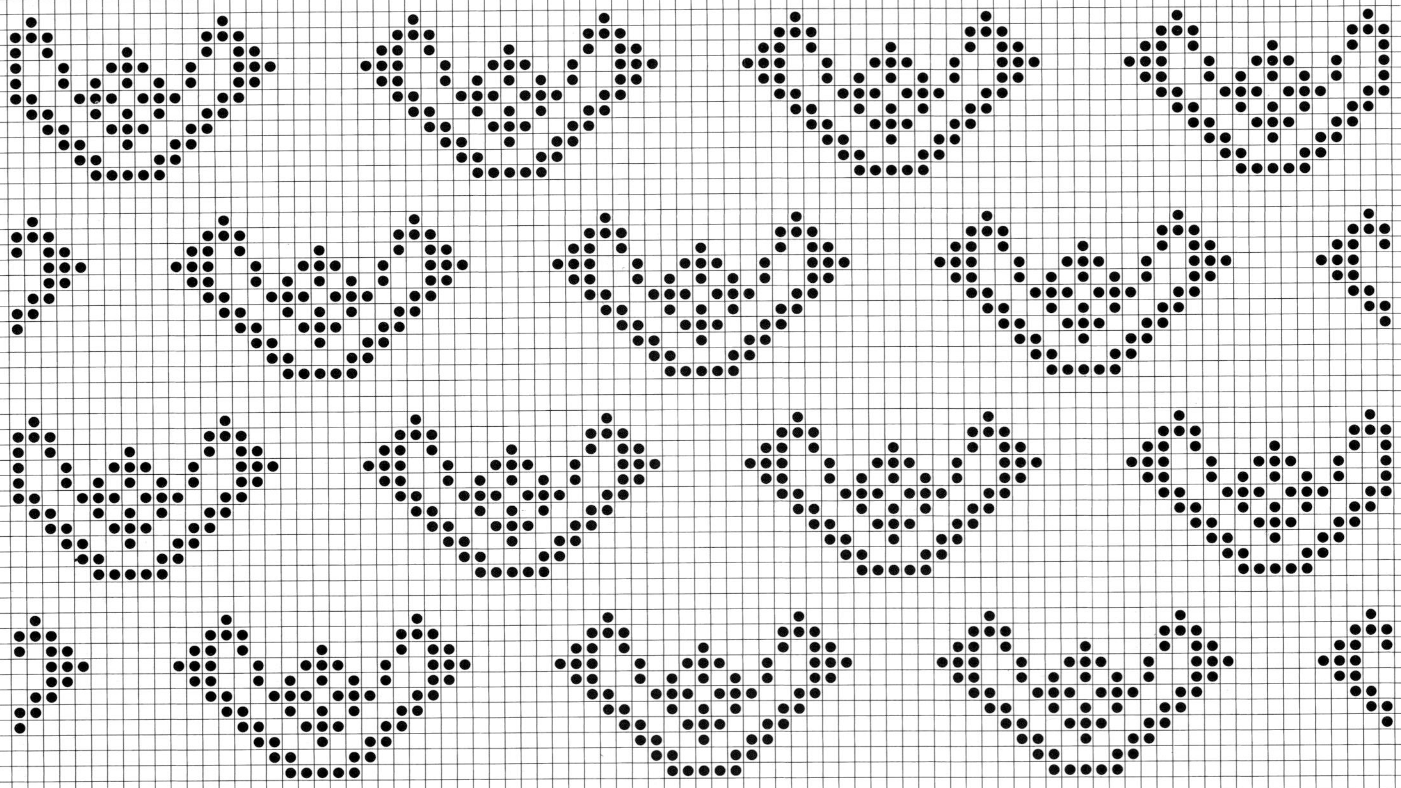

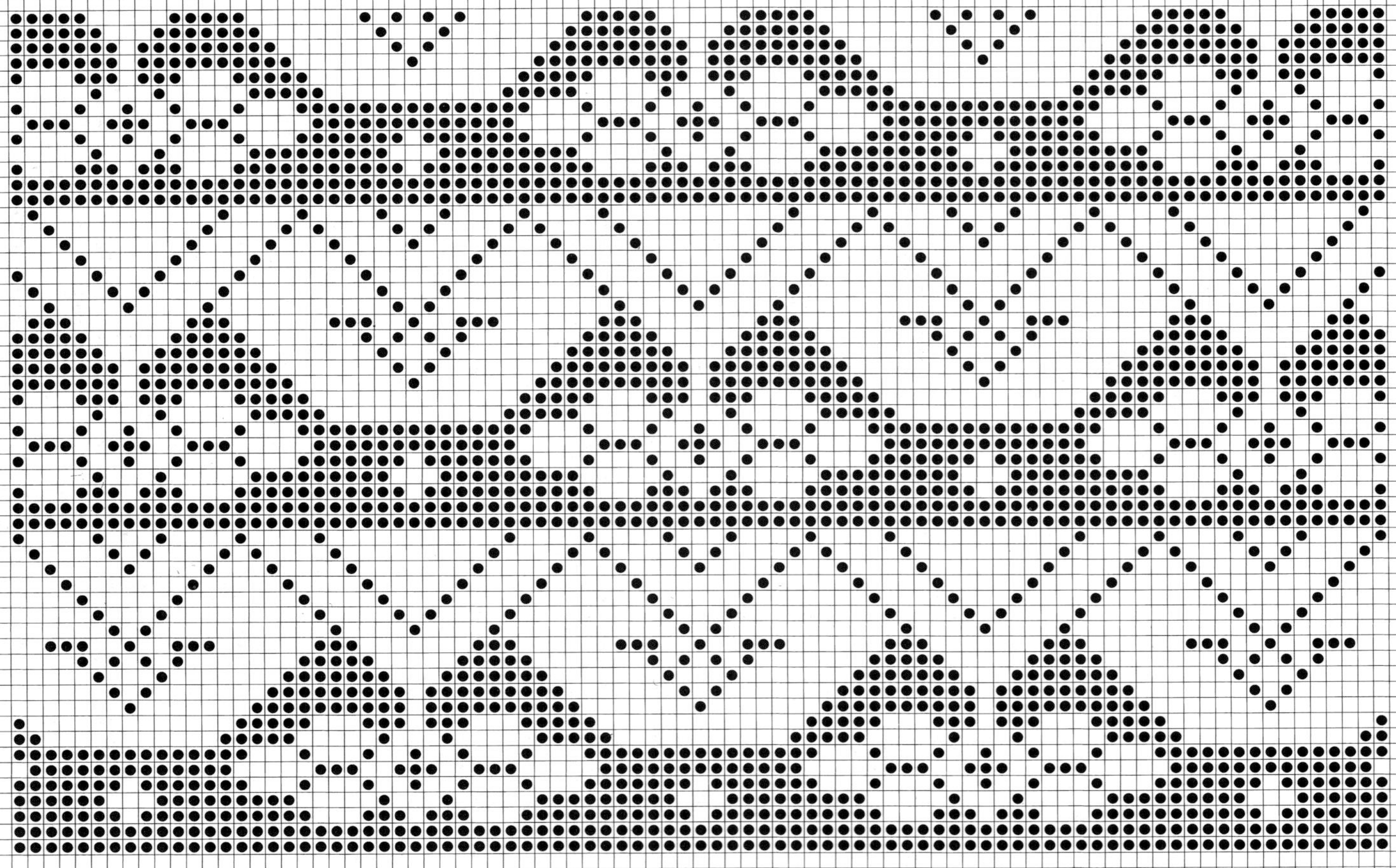

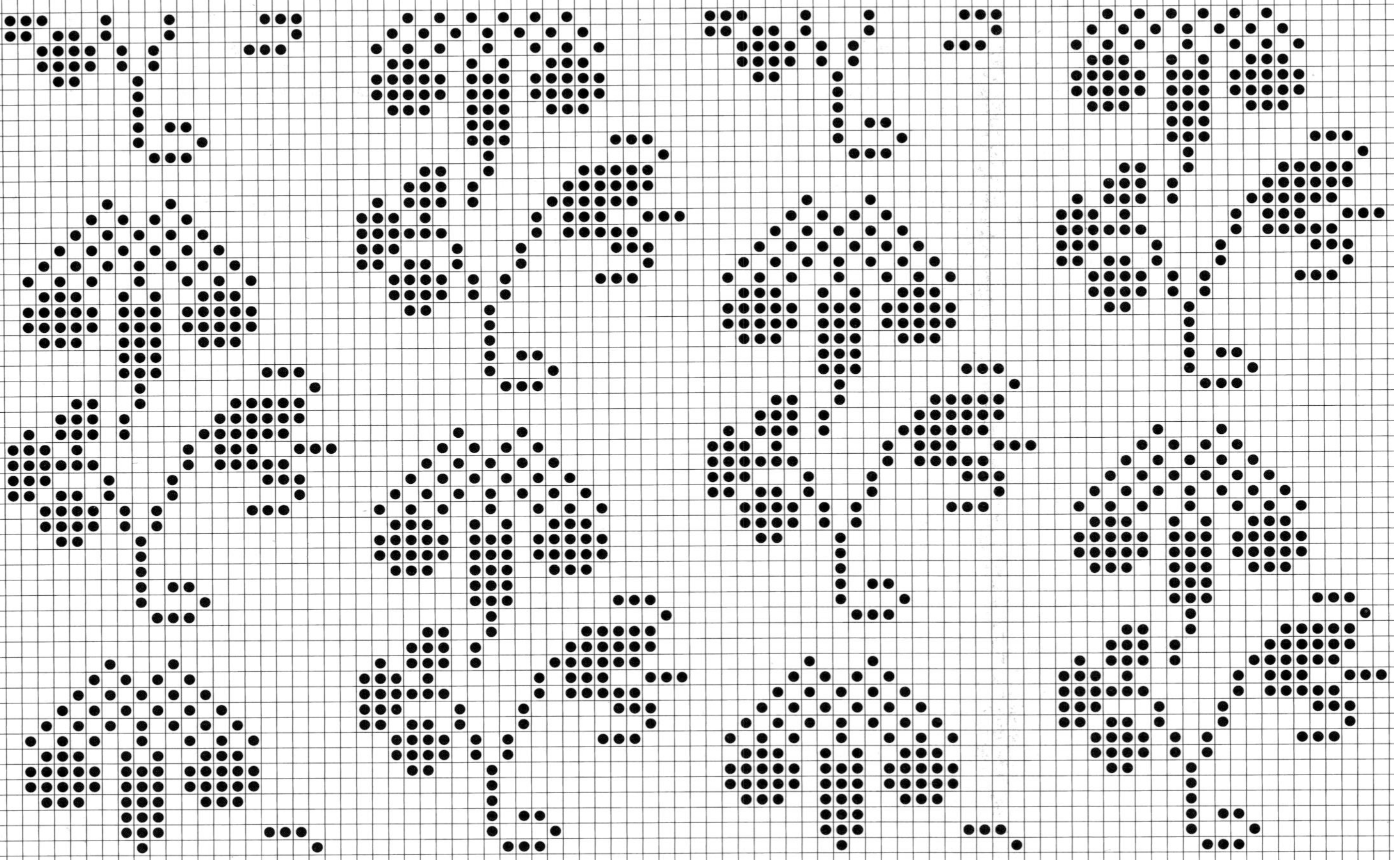

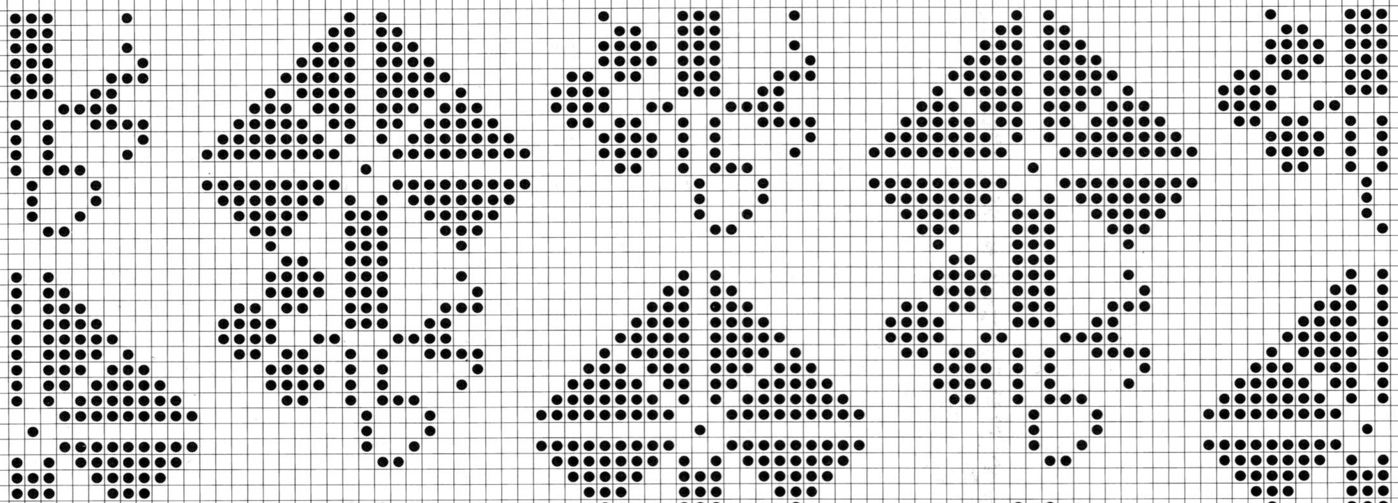

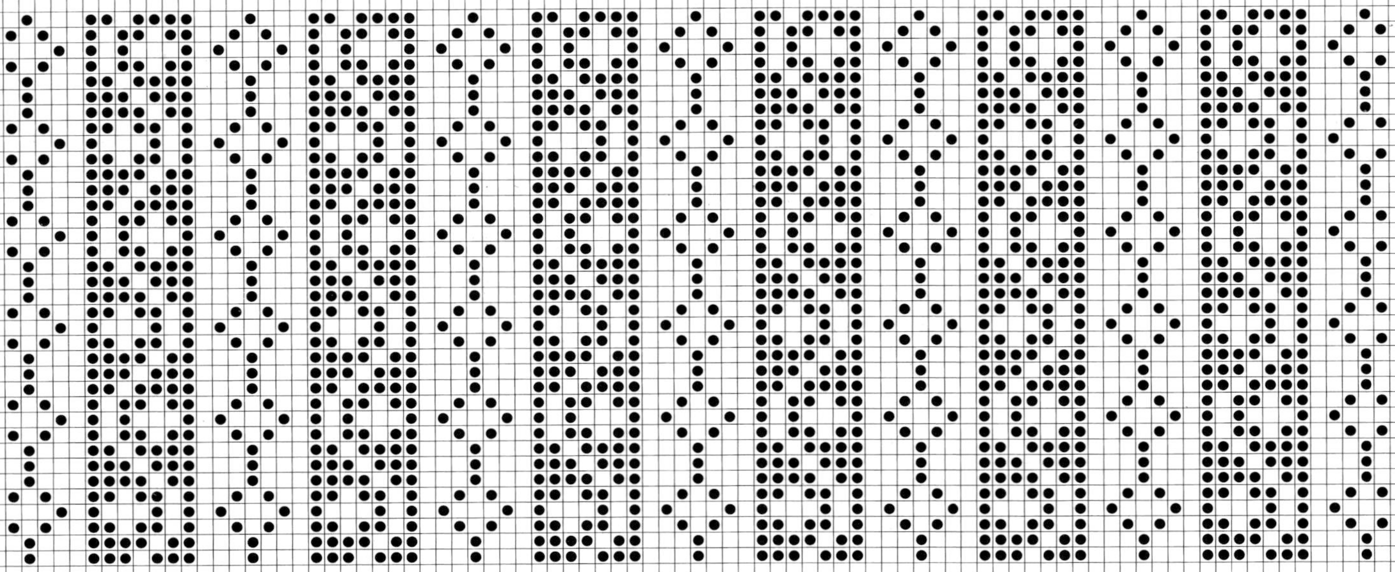

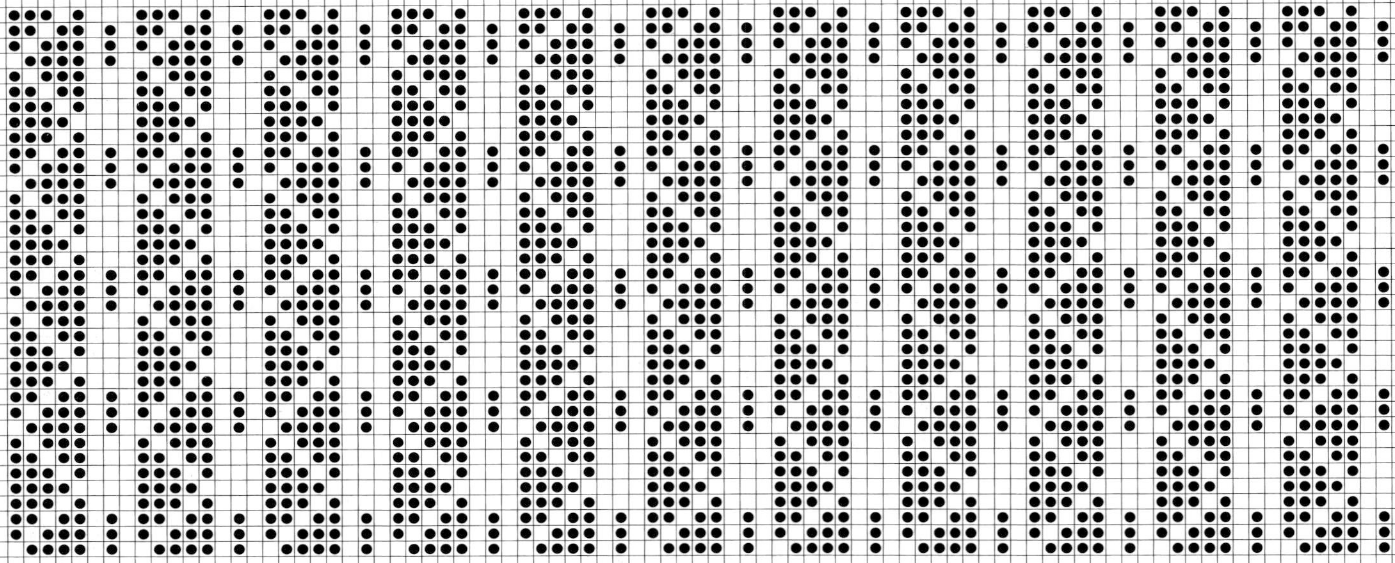

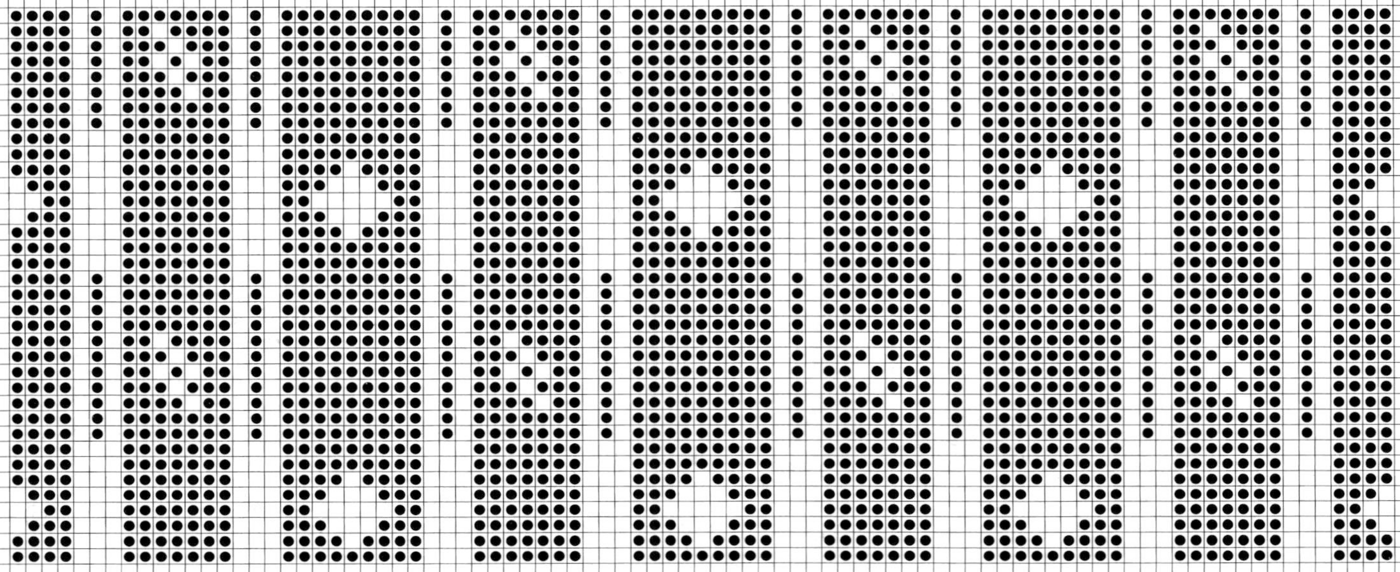

FINLAND

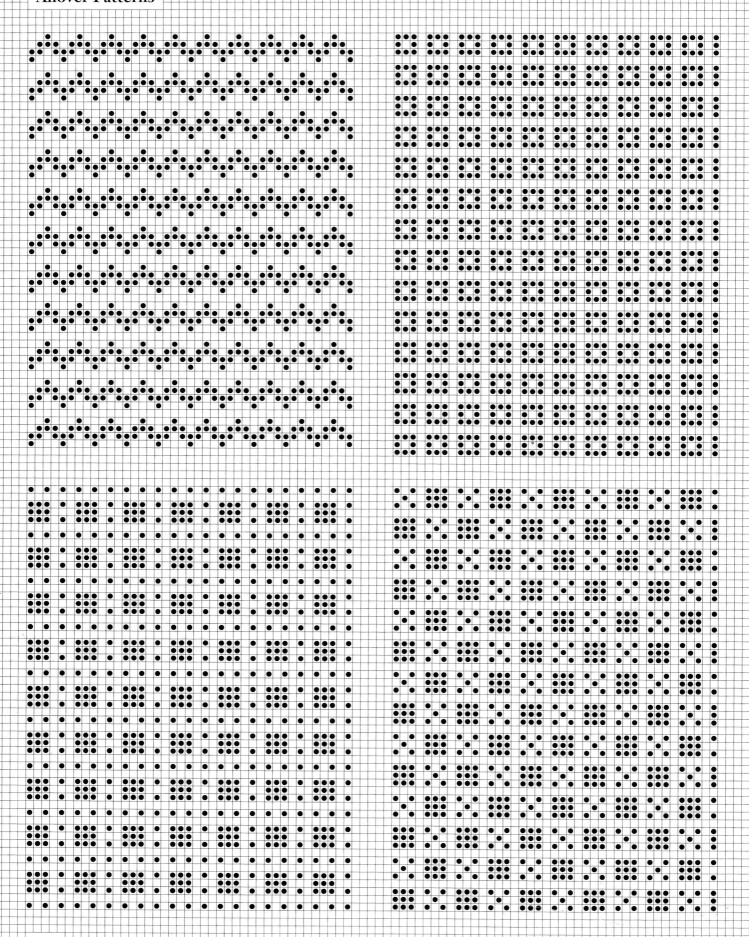

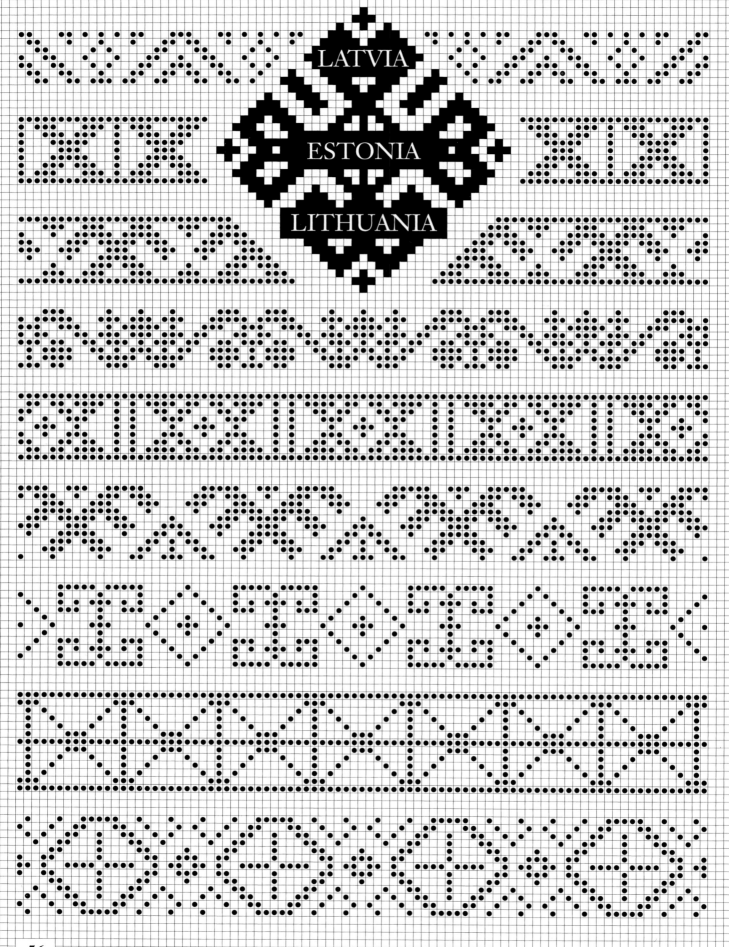

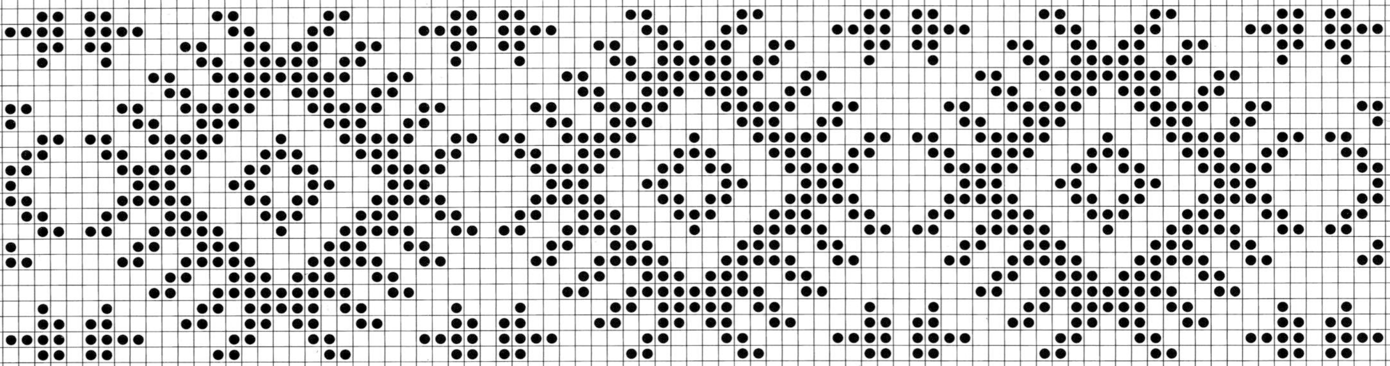

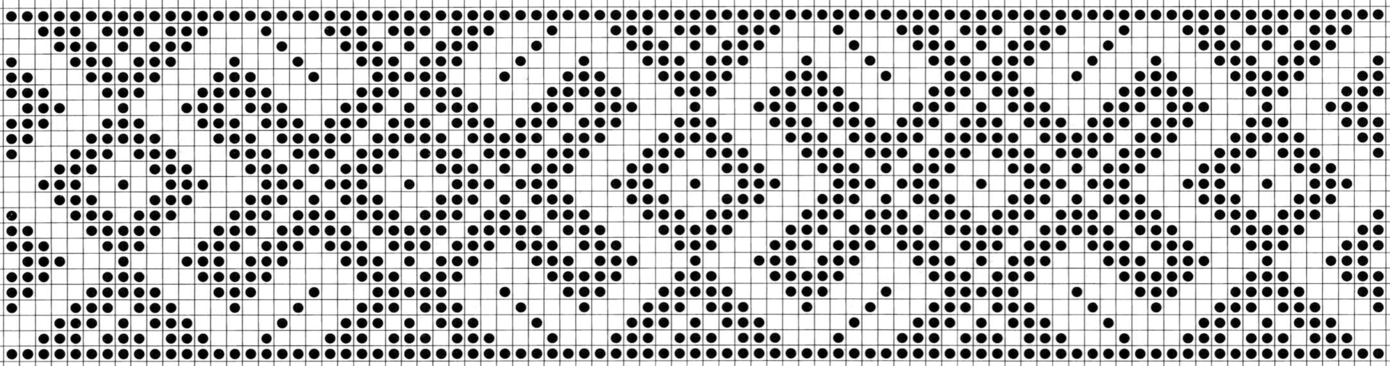

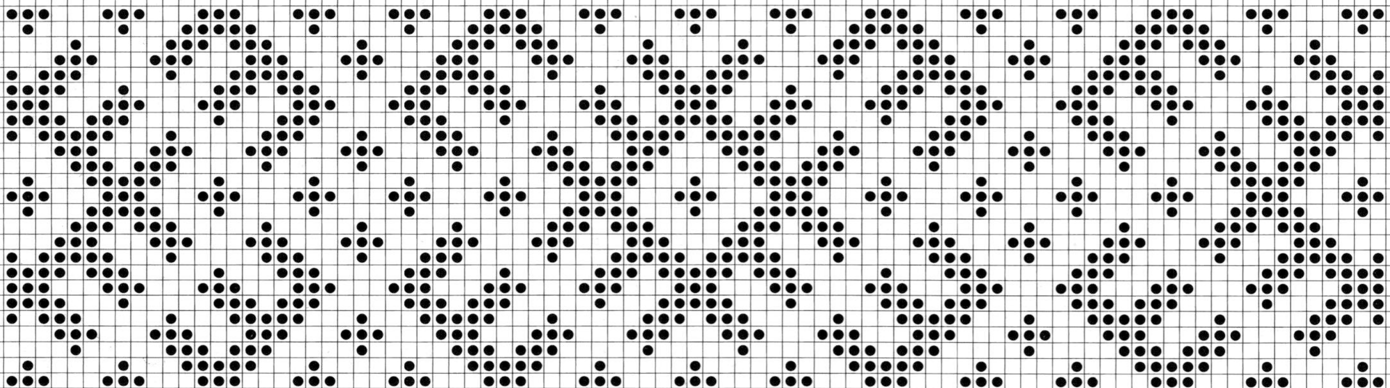

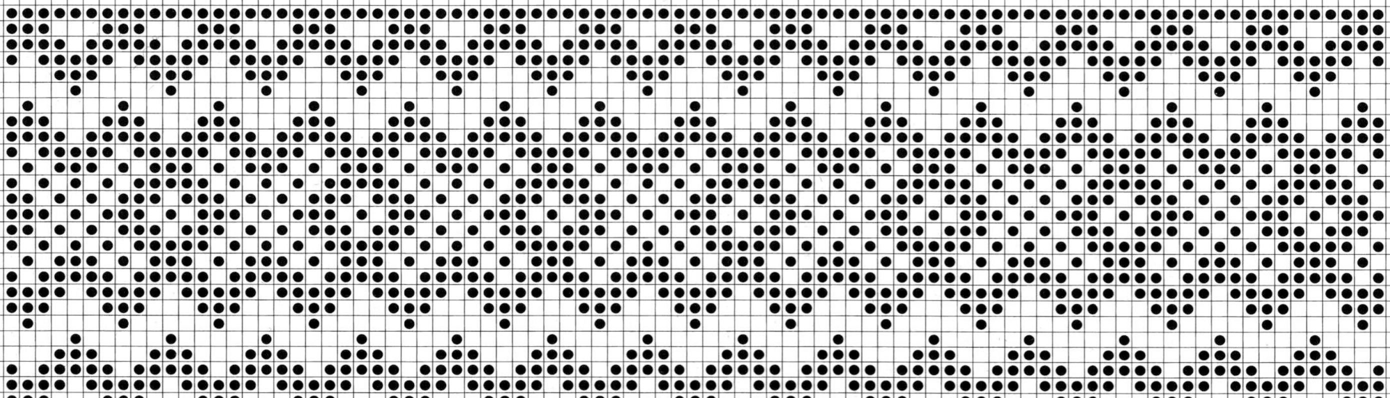

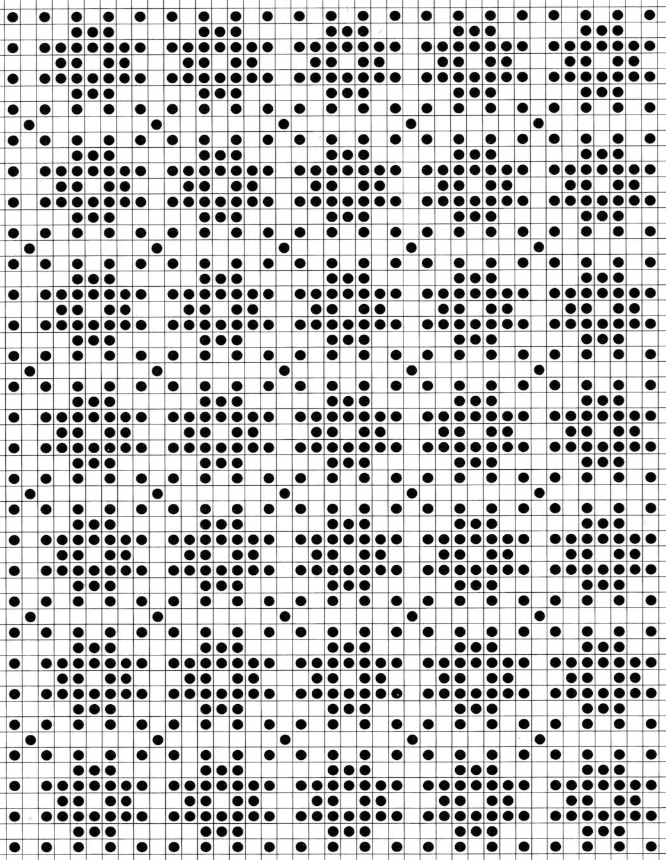

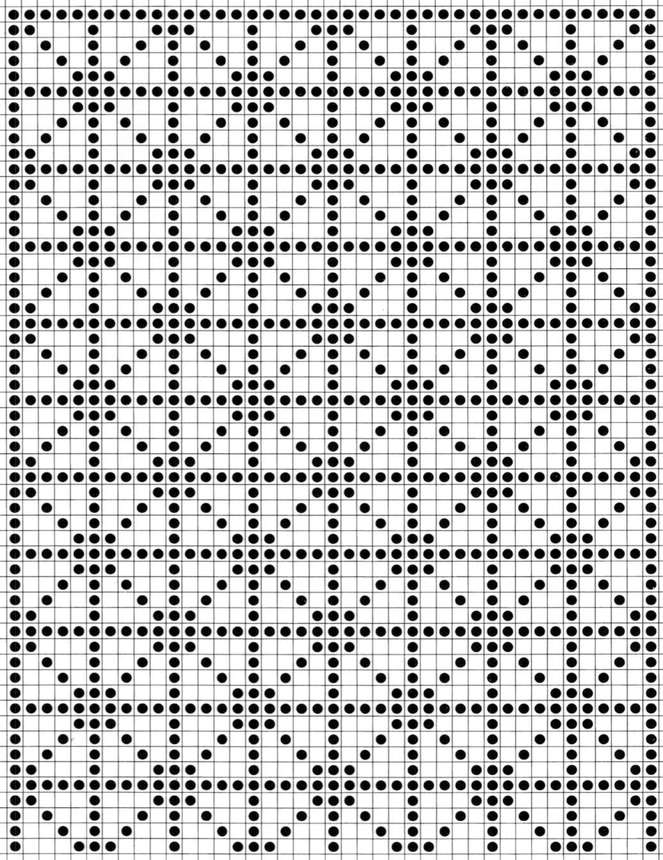

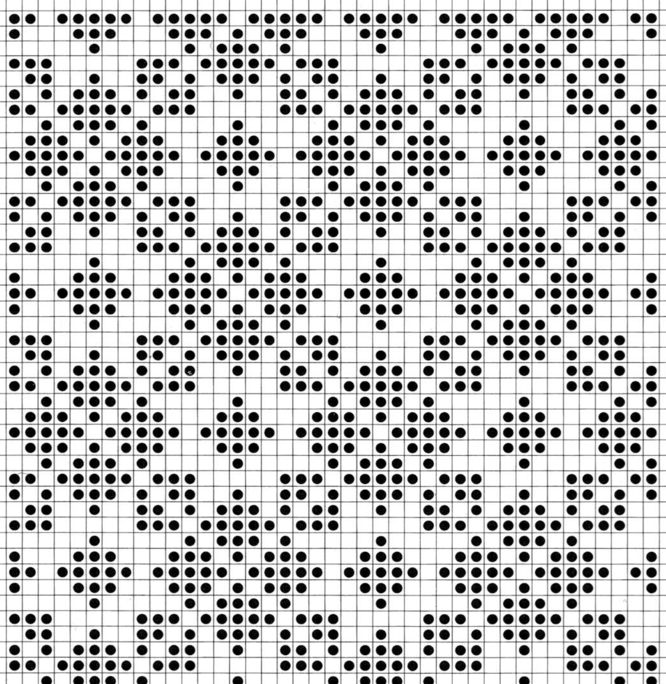

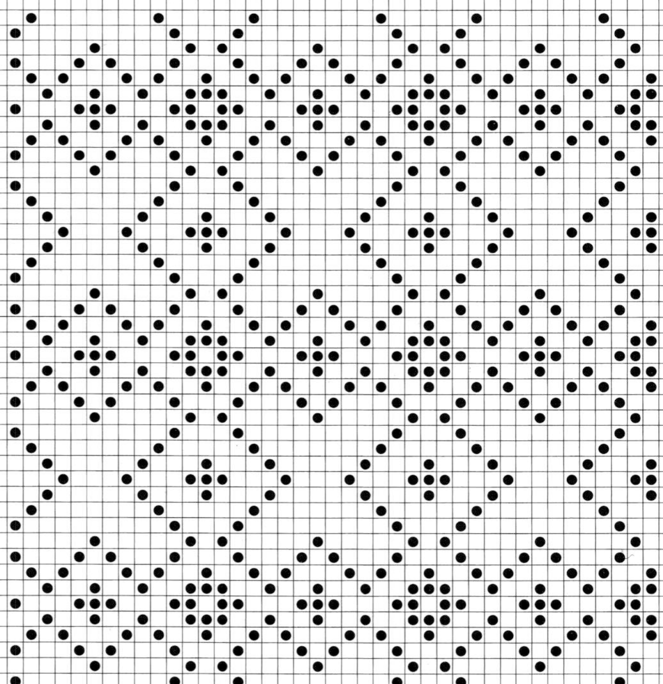

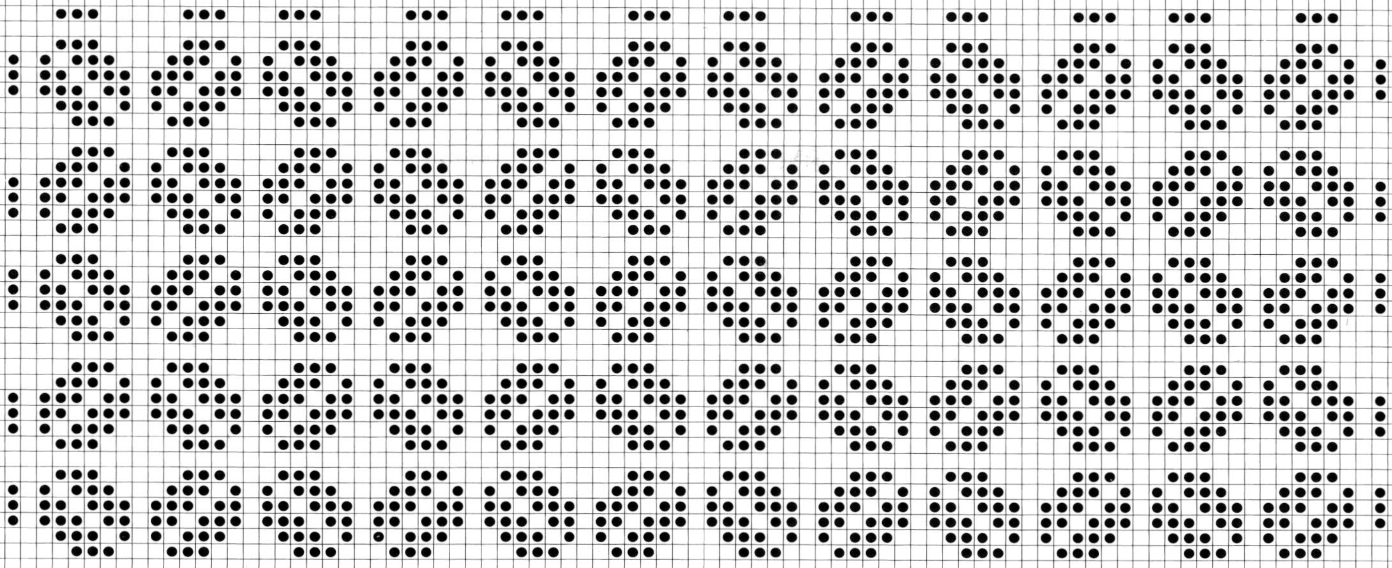

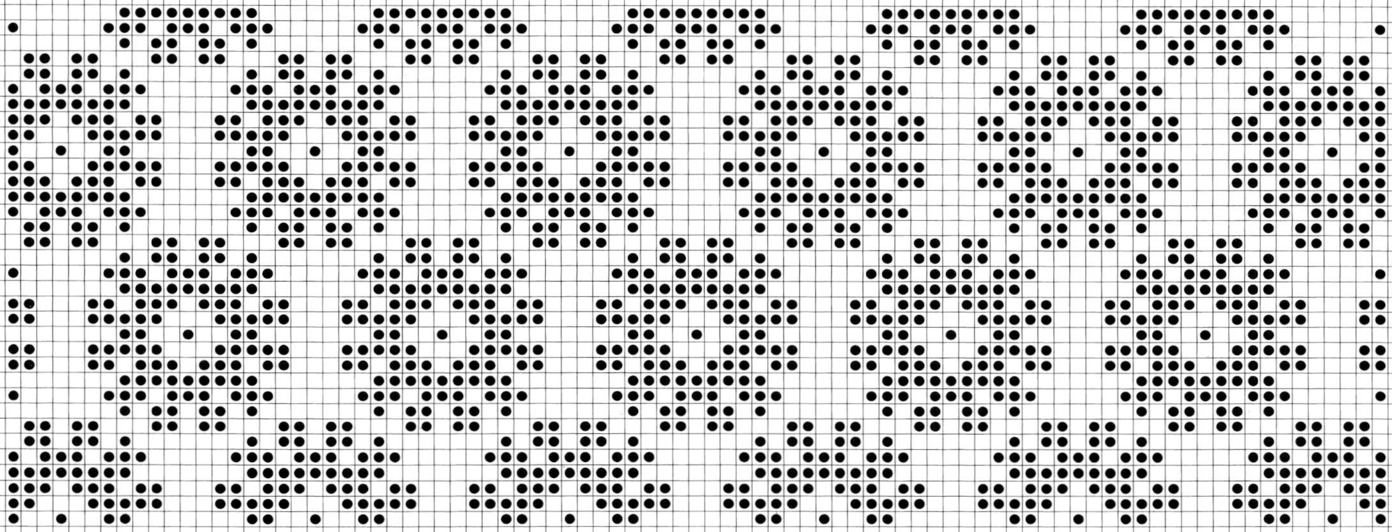

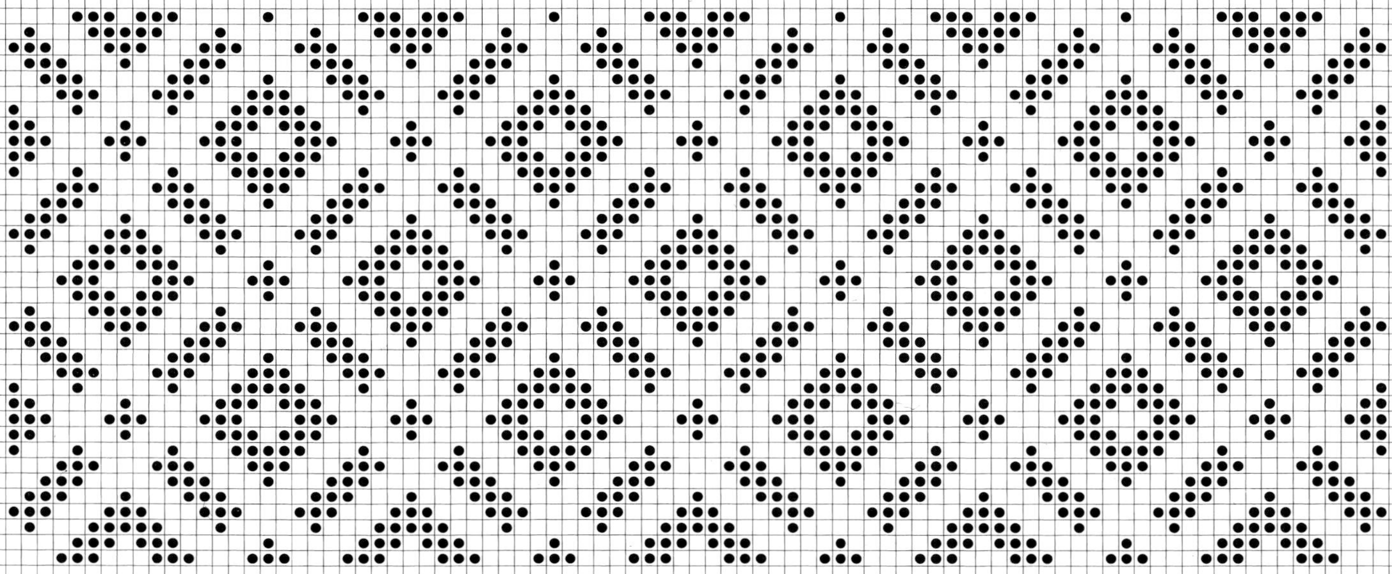

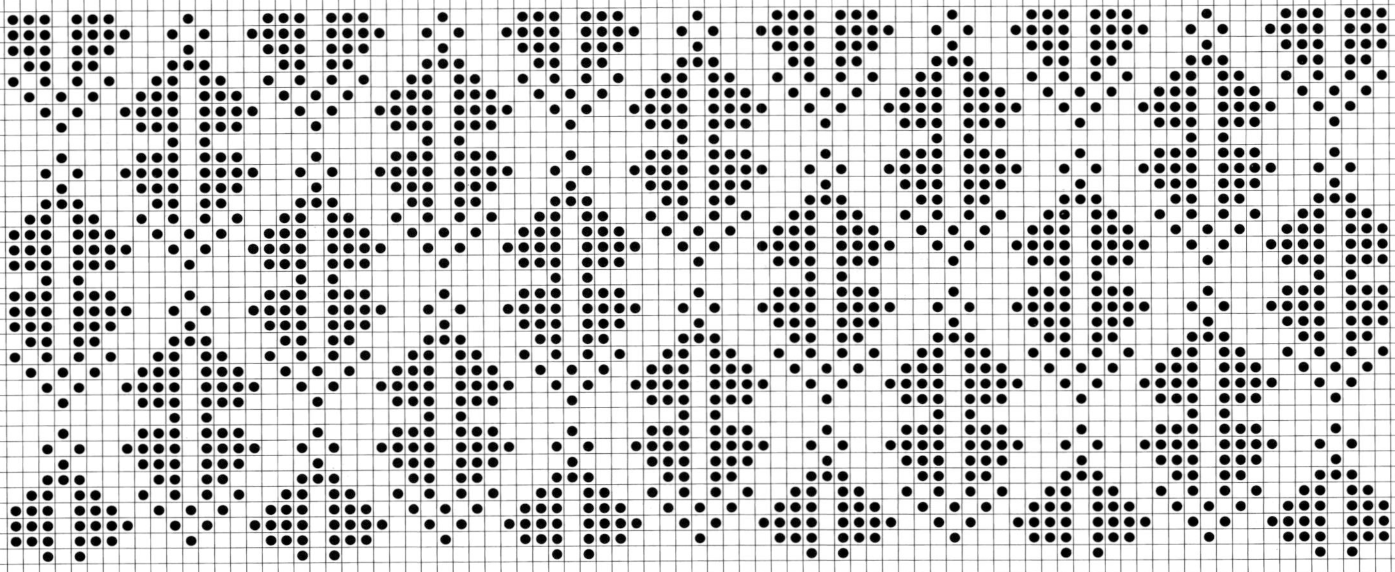

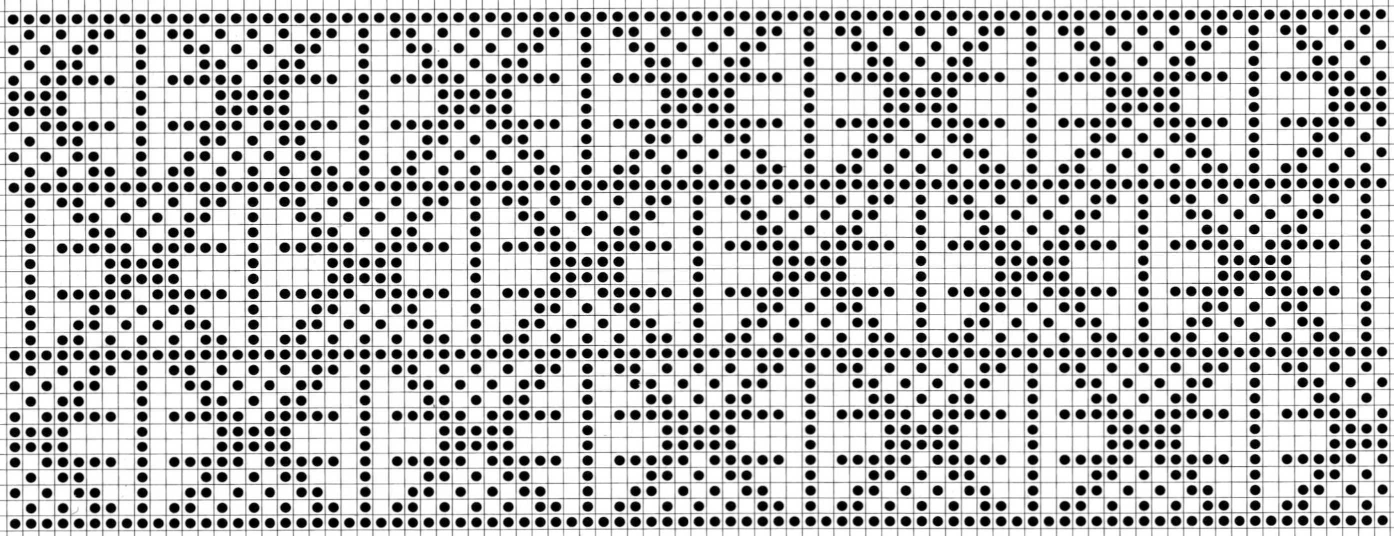

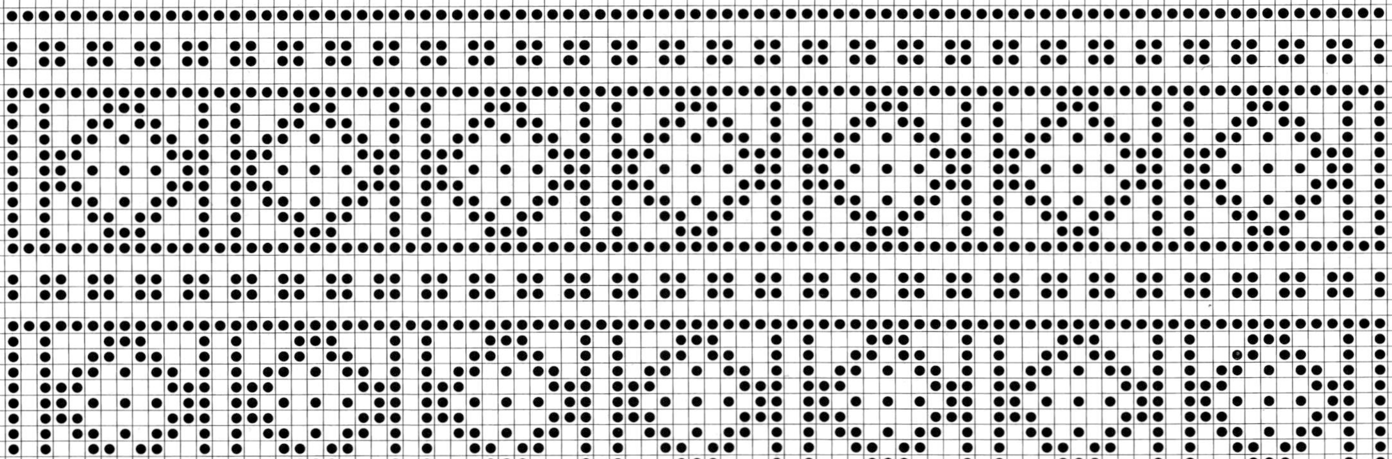

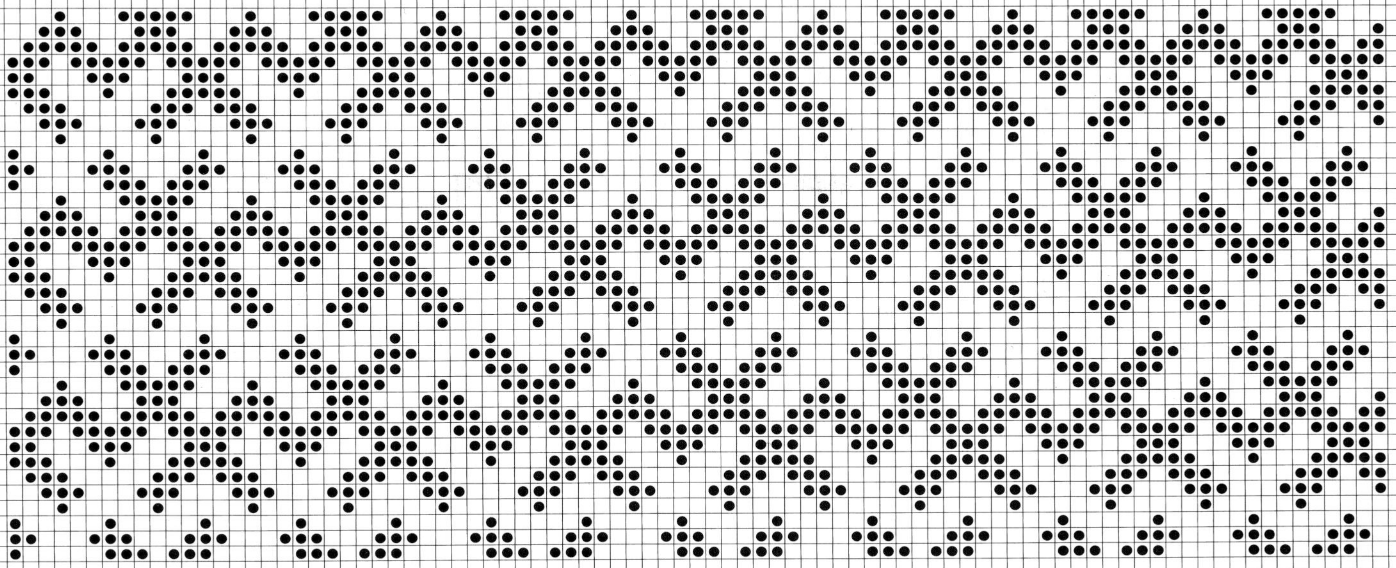

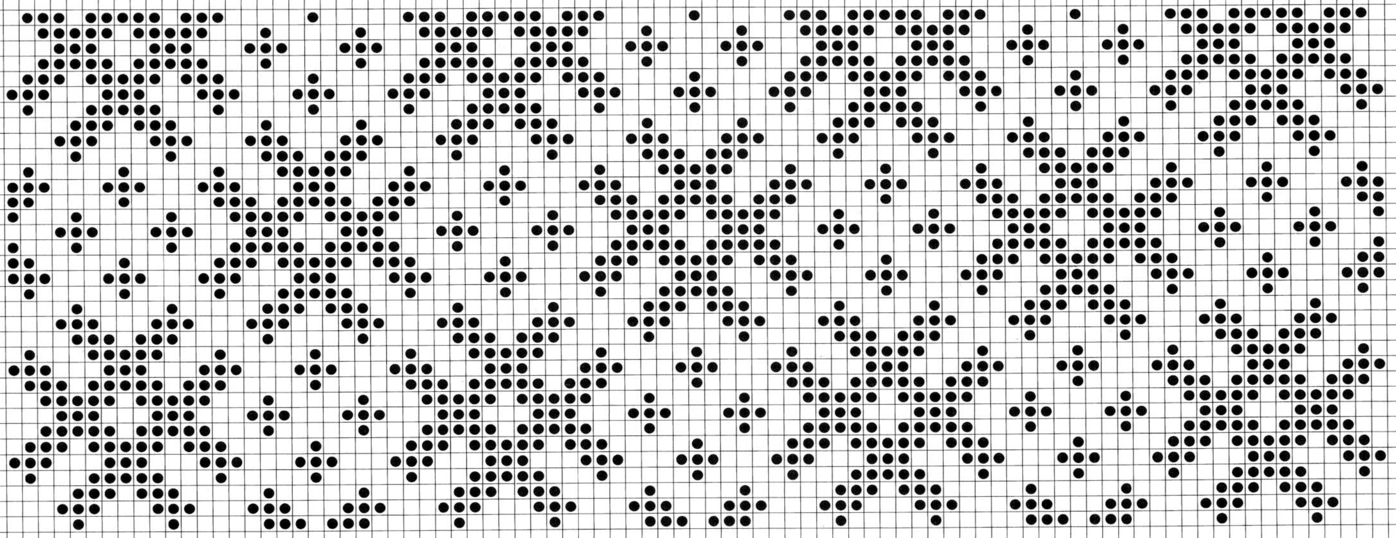

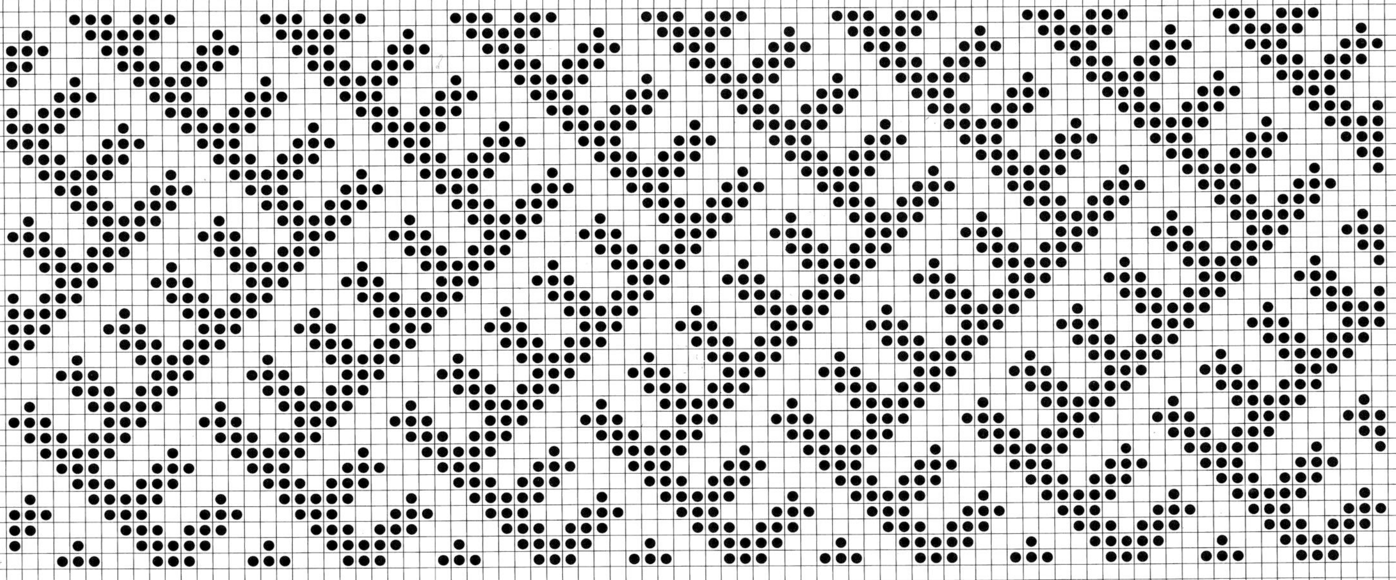

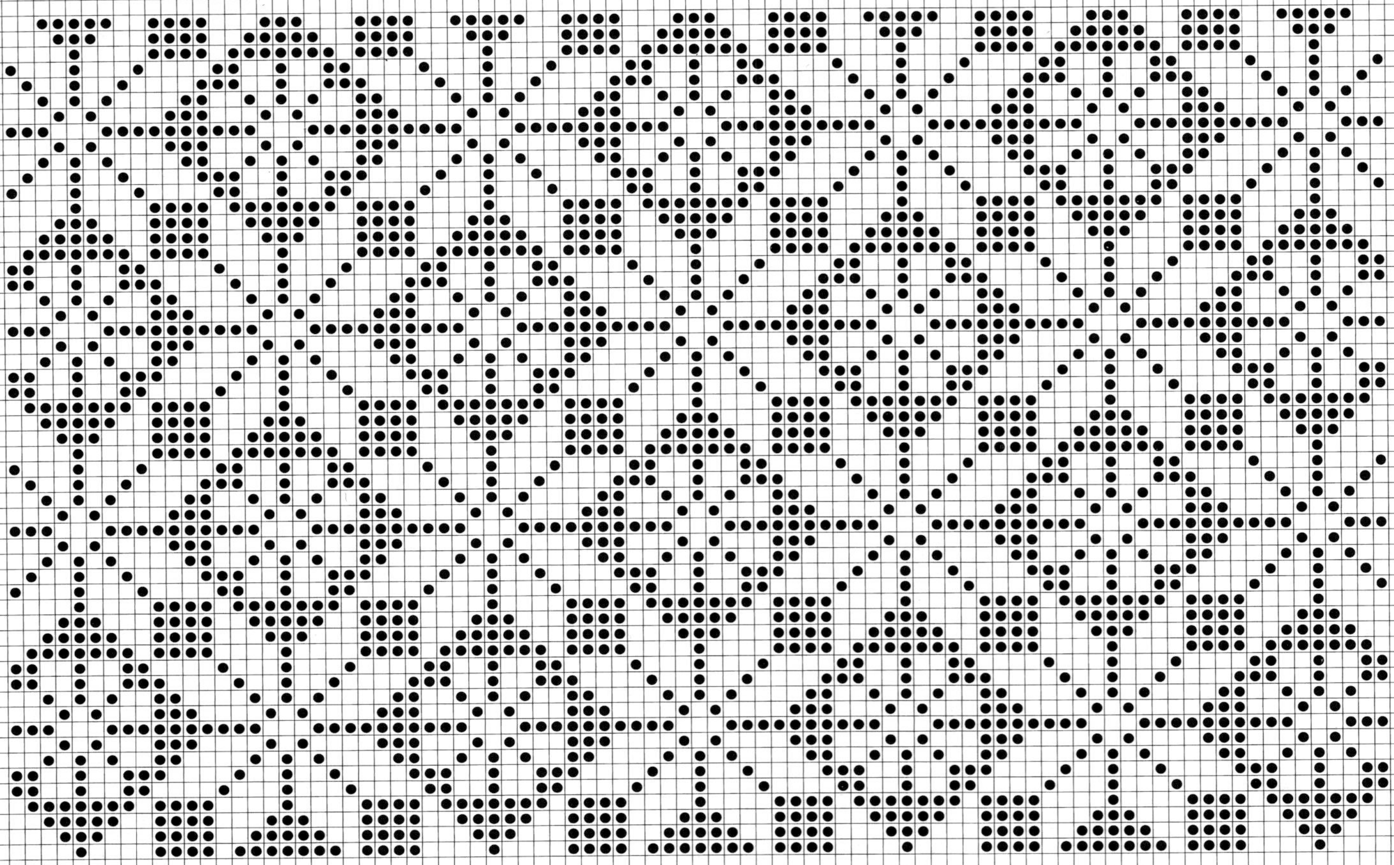

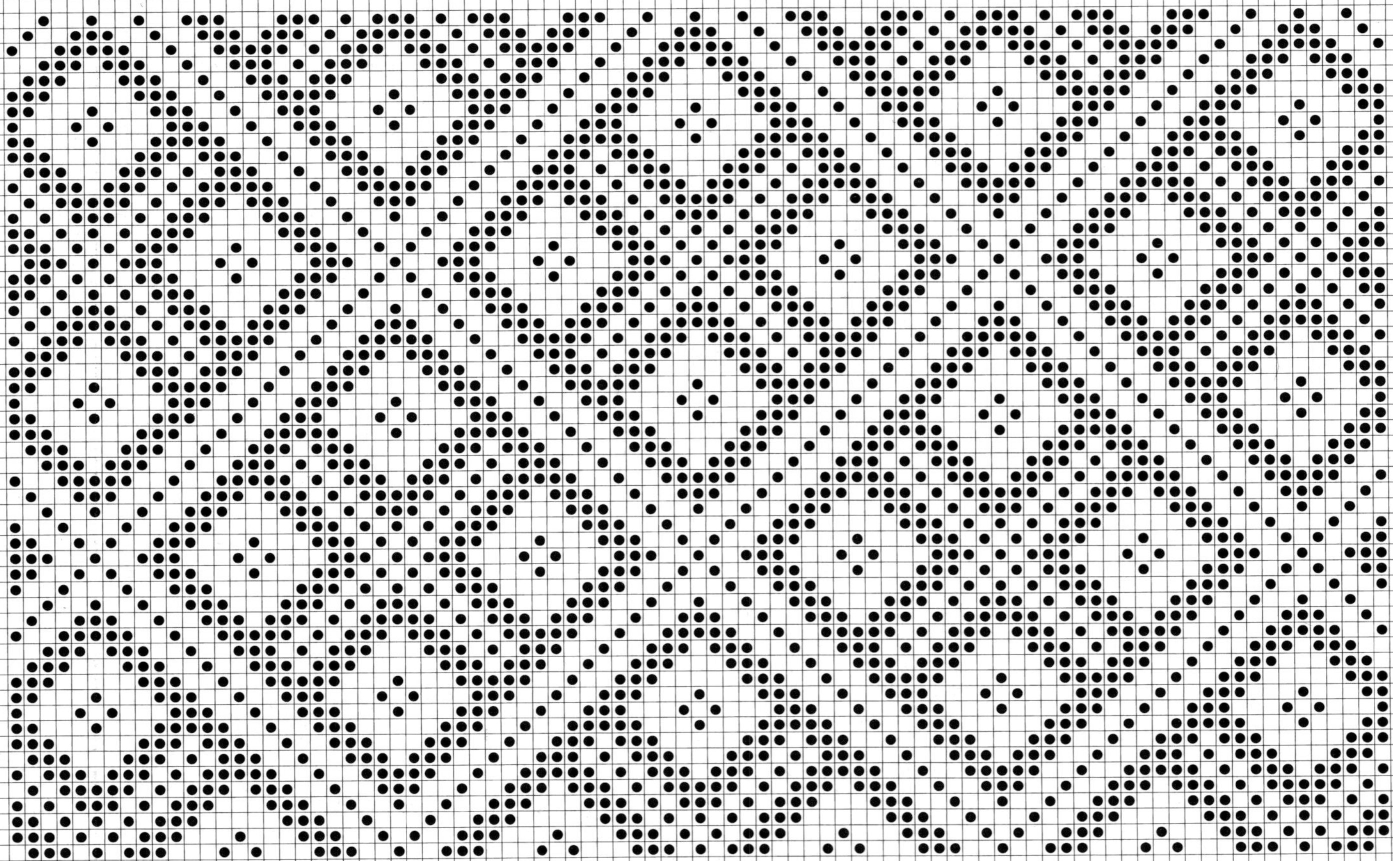

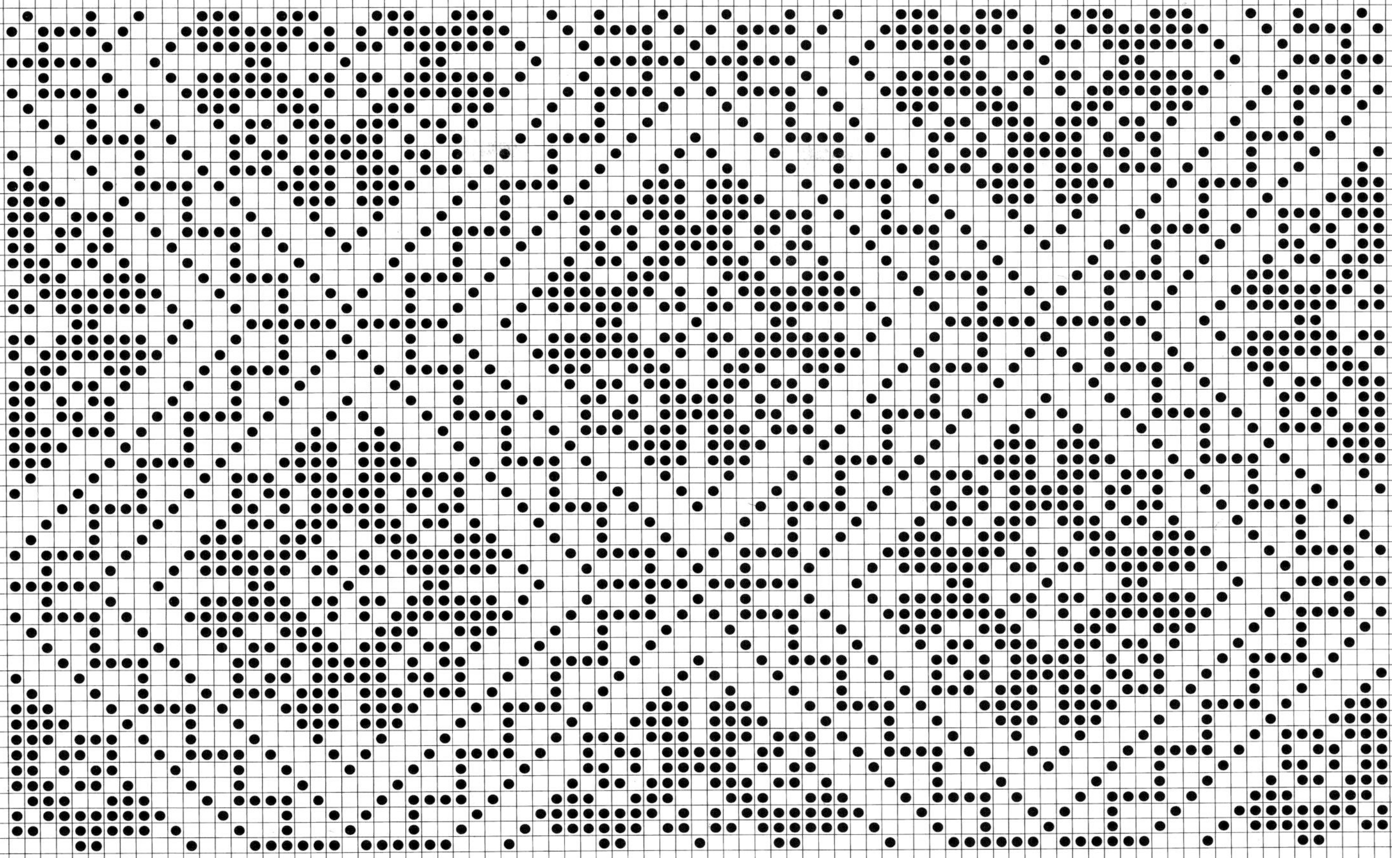

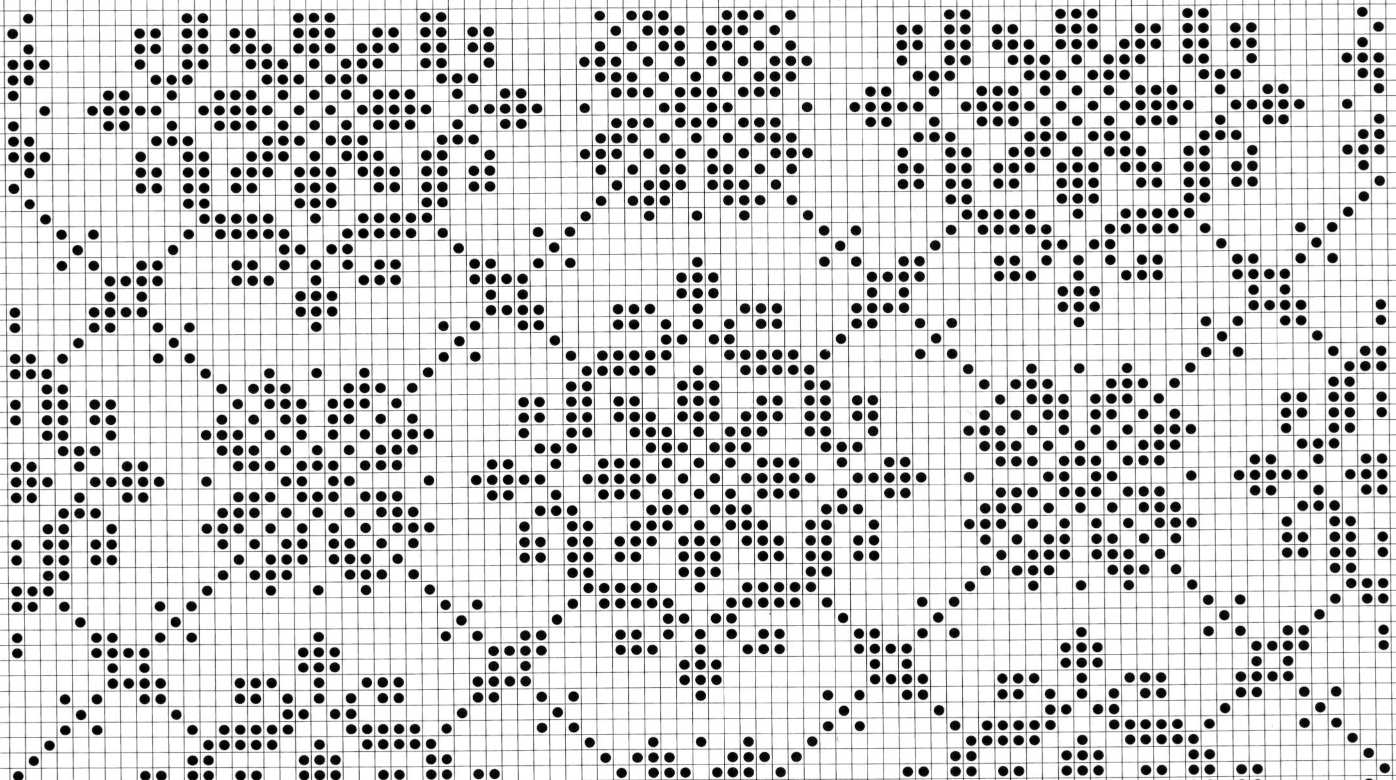

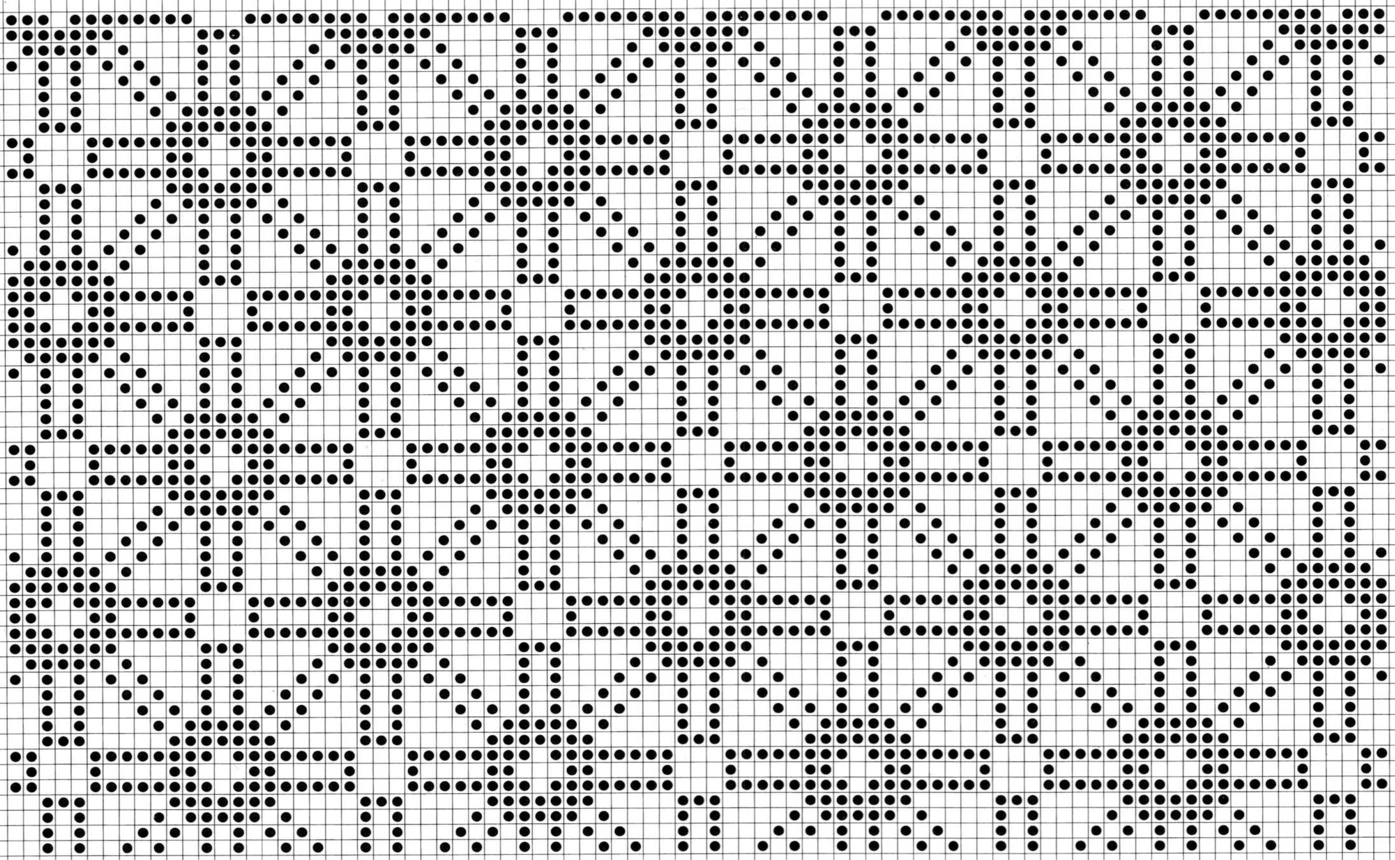

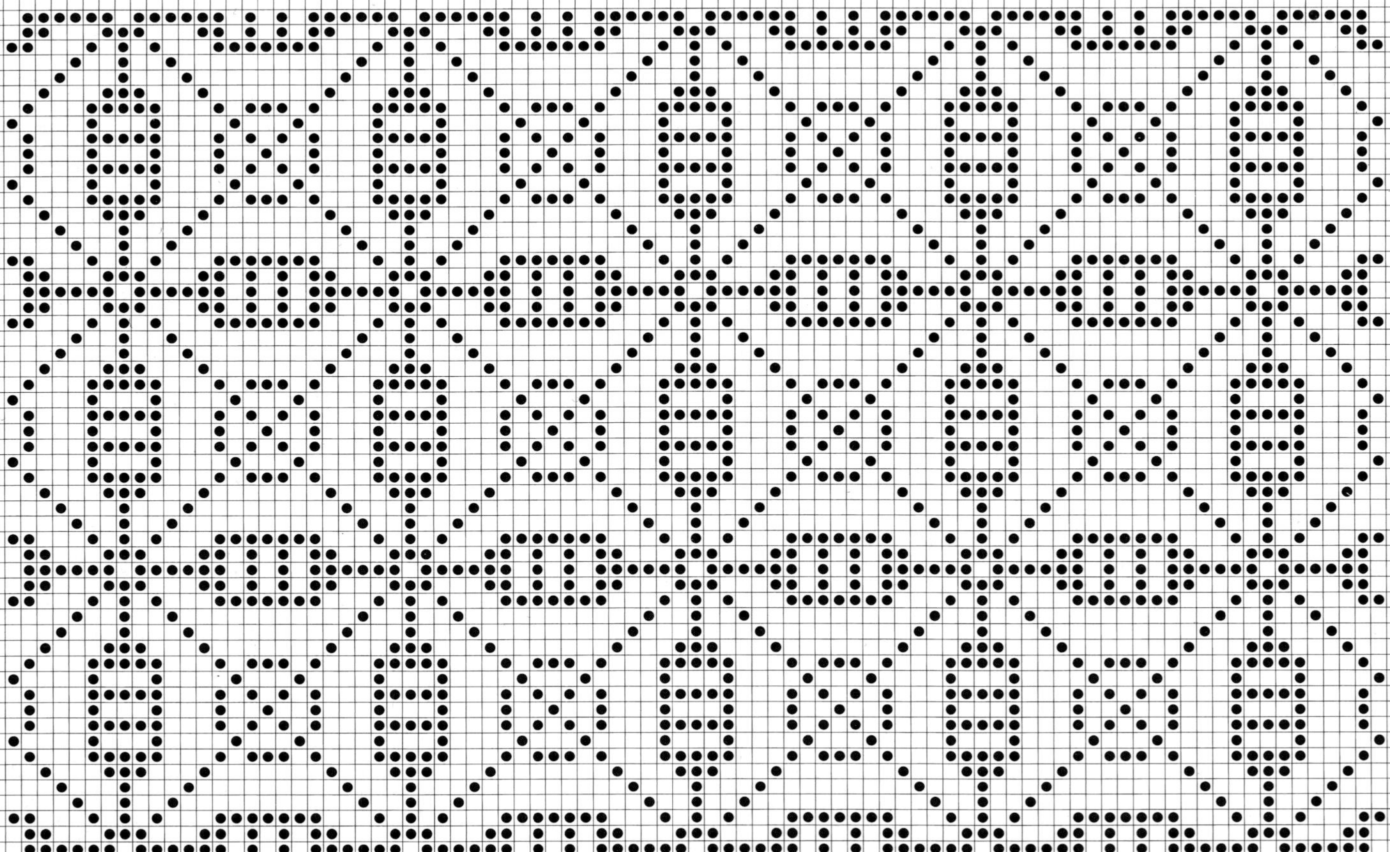

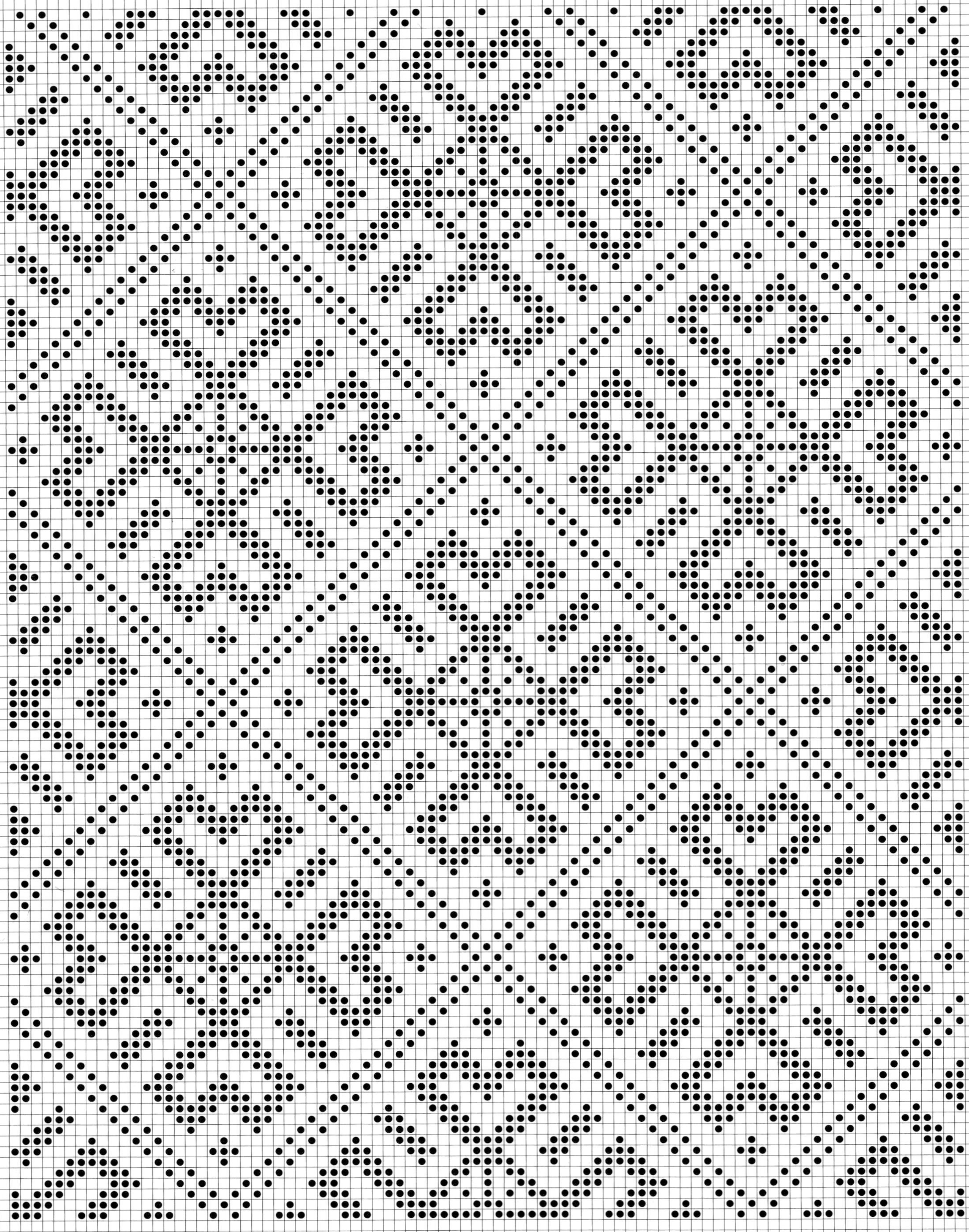

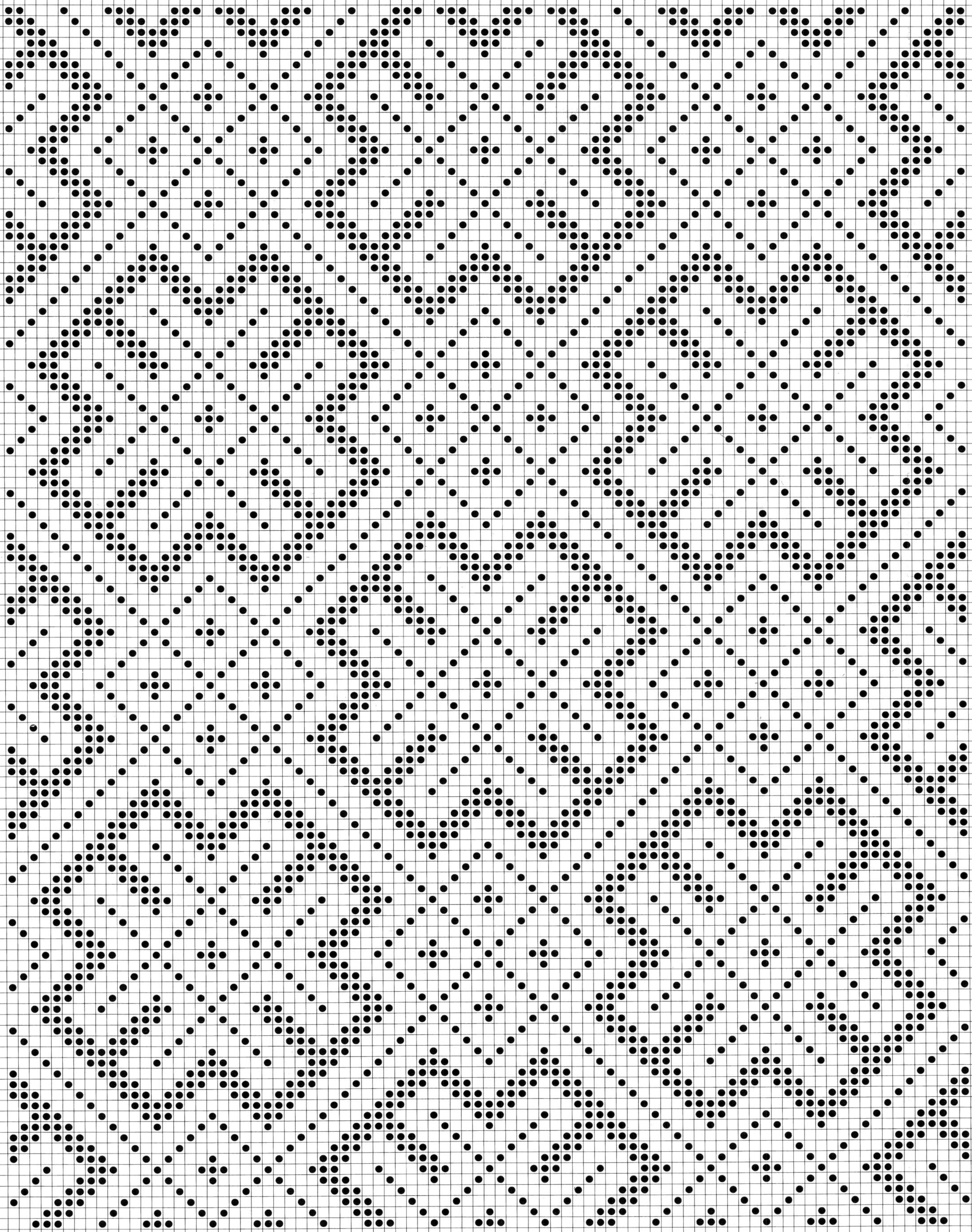

RUSSIA

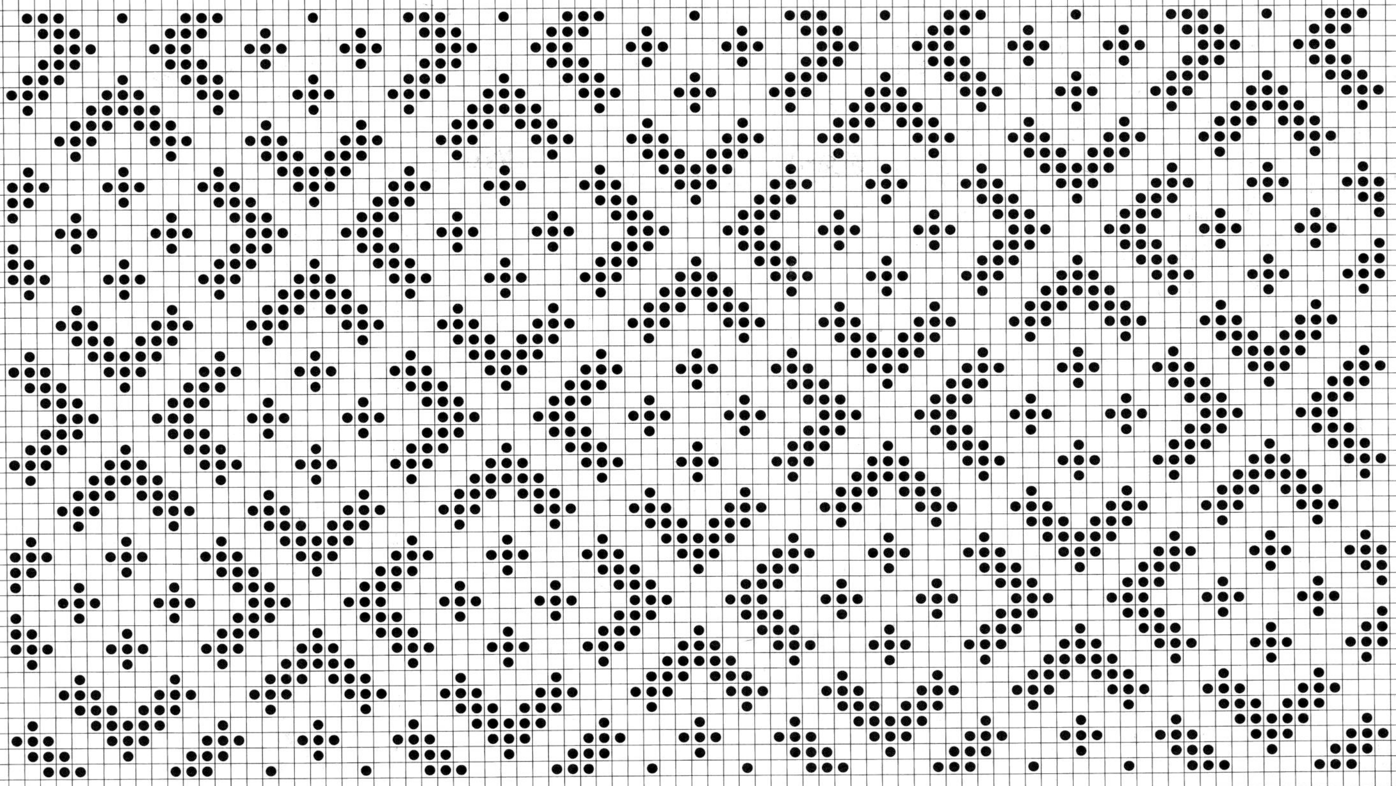

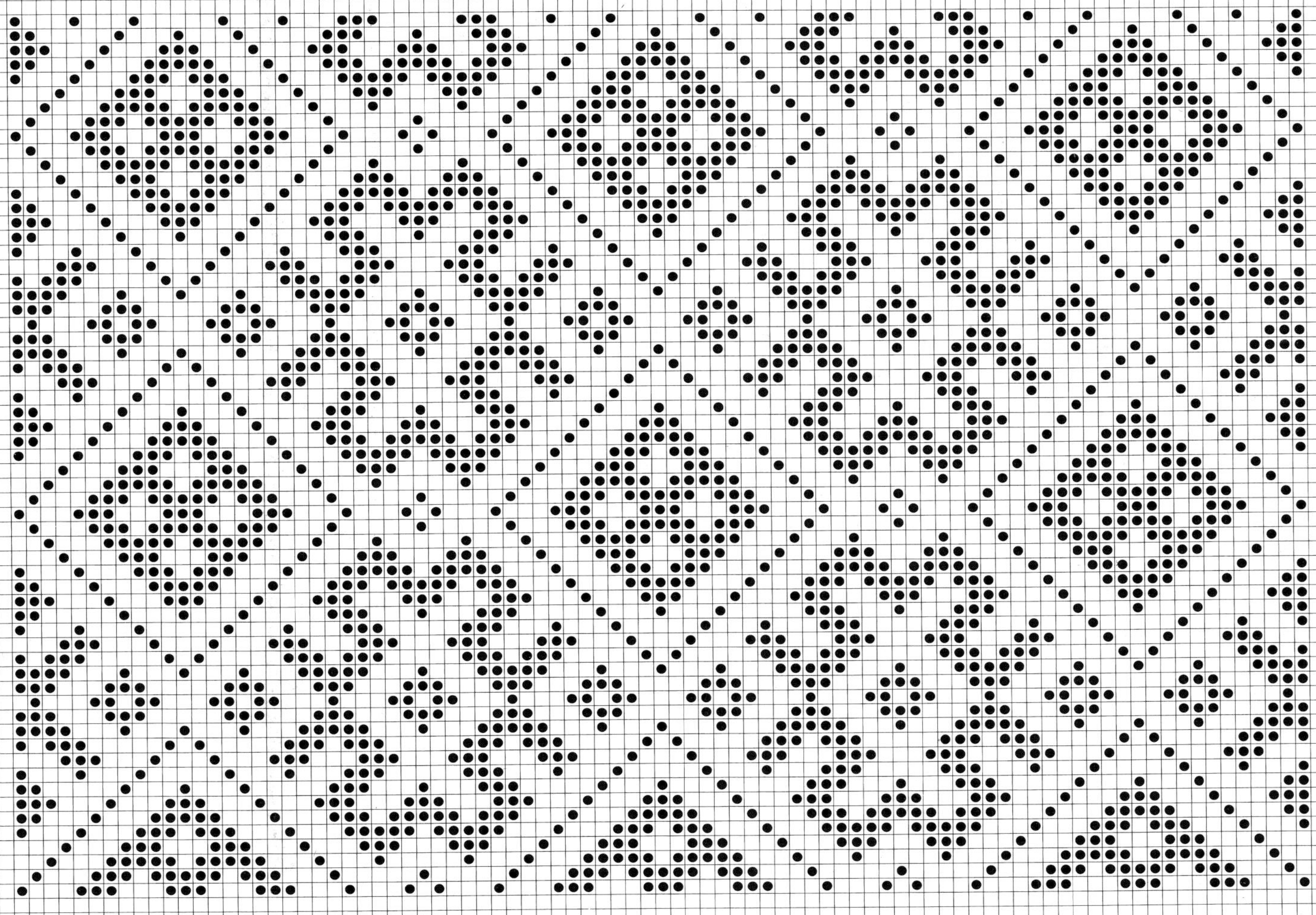

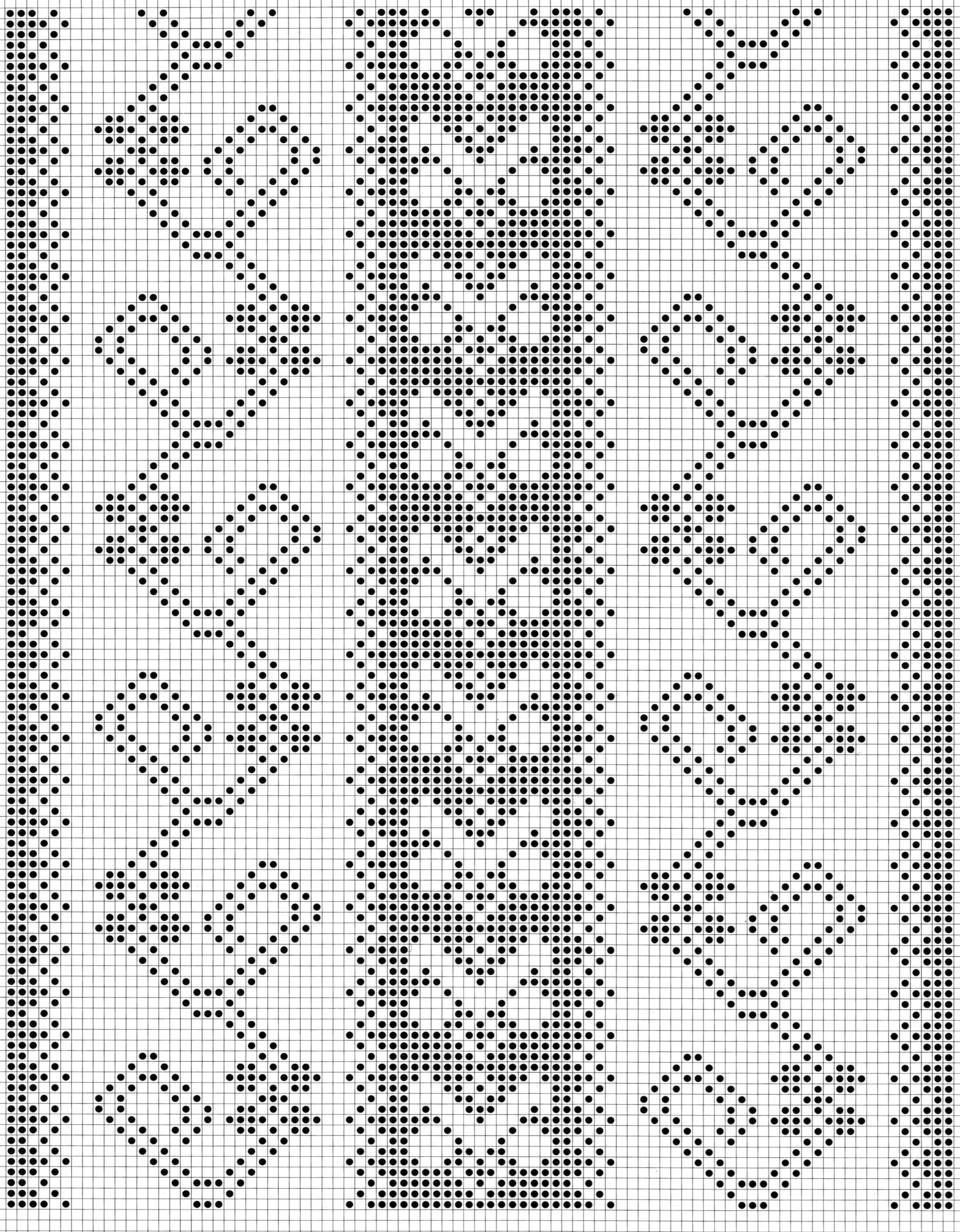

SOUTH AMERICA

SOUTH AMERICA

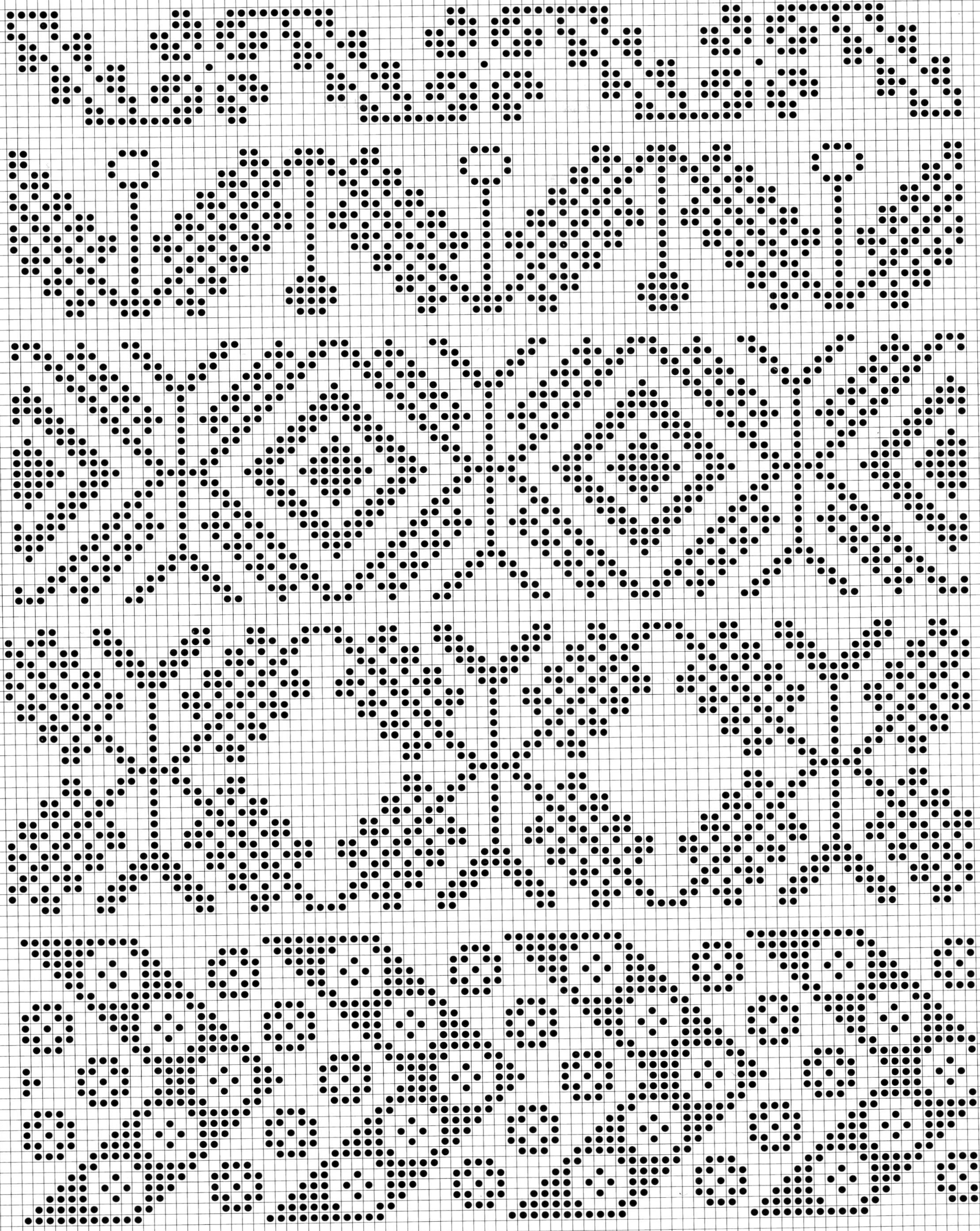

Adapted Patterns

Many old knitting patterns were adapted from other textiles, such as weaving and embroidery, and as a knitter and enthusiastic pattern collector, I take great delight in carrying on this tradition. However, I have widened the process to include whatever I see on my travels, be it textiles, architecture, jewellery, pottery . . . anything. Some patterns are perfect for knitting technique and require little alteration.

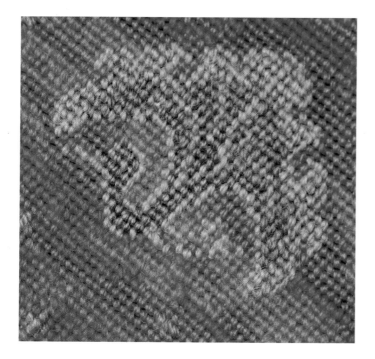

The Celtic "key" patterns from ancient manuscripts and stonework on pages 80 and 86 were simply graphed out directly. The same applies to the patterns from Japanese Sashiko stitching on page 107. Others require adaptation to a varying degree, such as the patterns in the Caucasian section, which were largely taken from carpets.

The process of adaptation can always include scope for personal creativity. The large allover pattern on page 87 for example, was taken from quite a basic Celtic key pattern. I extended it, created the diamond spaces, and filled them with a cross which I designed myself in a Celtic style. This elaboration can be both rewarding and fun.

We are surrounded by a treasure house of decoration, and I can recommend actively hunting out patterns in this way. In doing so, we are following the "magpie" instincts of keen knitters down the ages—an instinct which has contributed more to the historical development of our craft than any other single factor. Older Scottish knitters of my mother's generation have often told me of seeing a pattern while working away from home, and knitting it from memory as soon as they got the chance. It was in this way that patterns were spread by fisher girls around the British coastline, often with developments and changes. Today we travel further and faster, and the scope for pattern hunting is better than ever before. Try it and see.

Above & Left: These two stitched patterns are adapted from Far-Eastern imagery and show how versatile charted designs can be. I worked the motifs in hand-dyed silks on backgrounds of Alice Starmore® *Hebridean 2 Ply*.

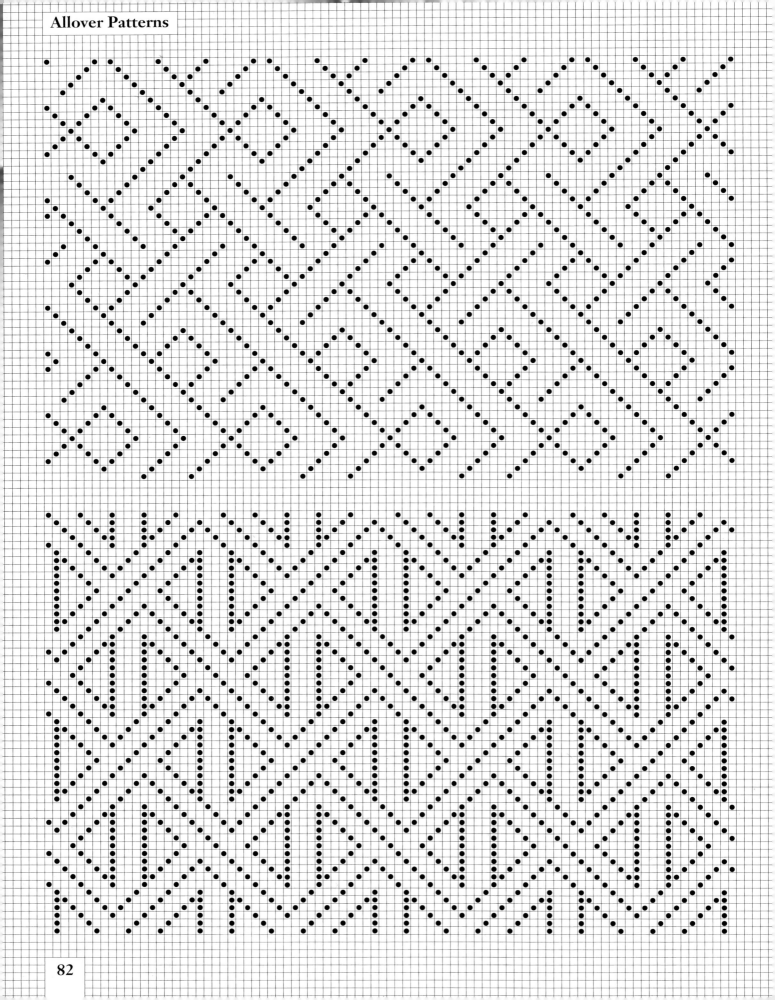

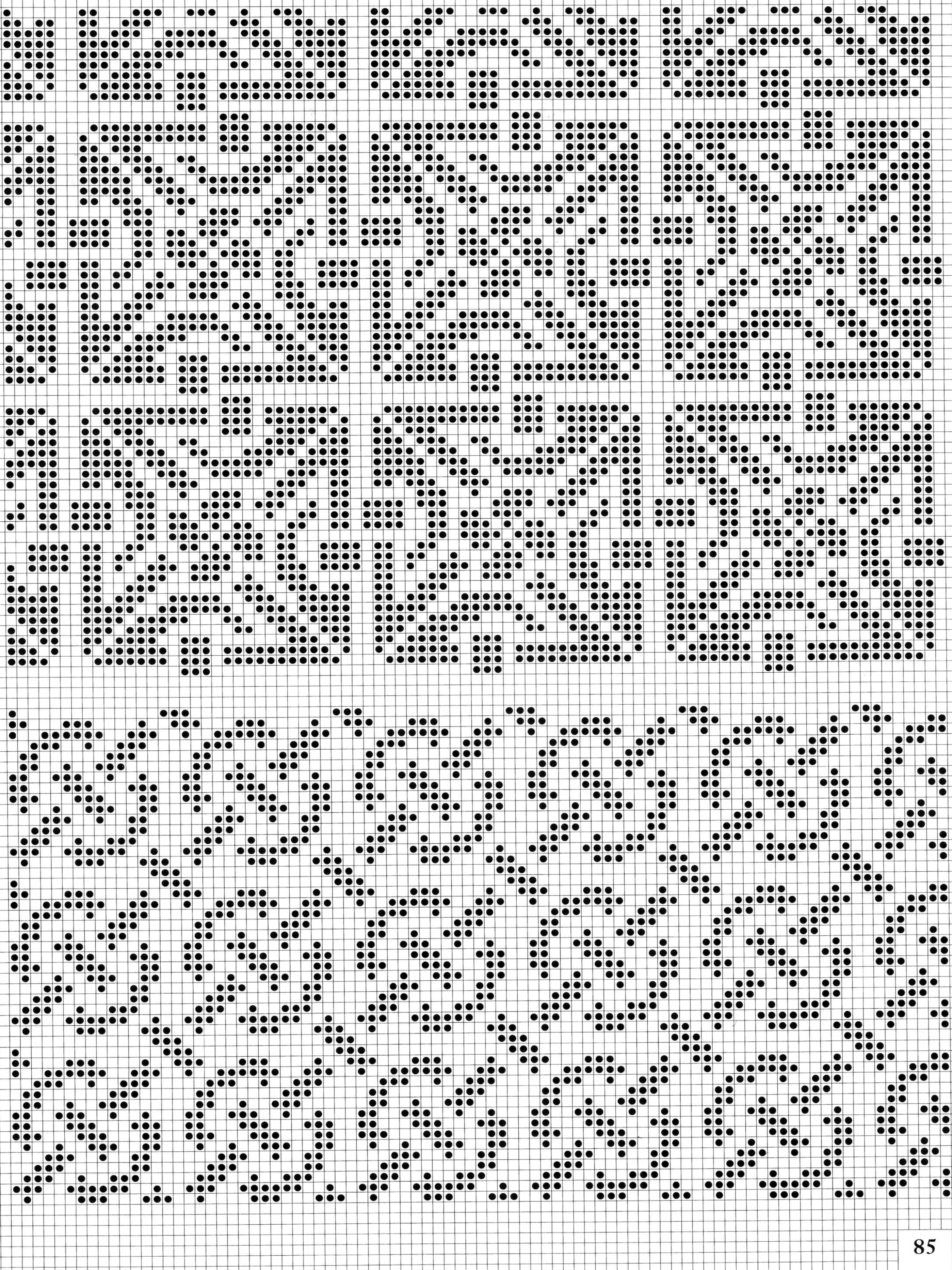

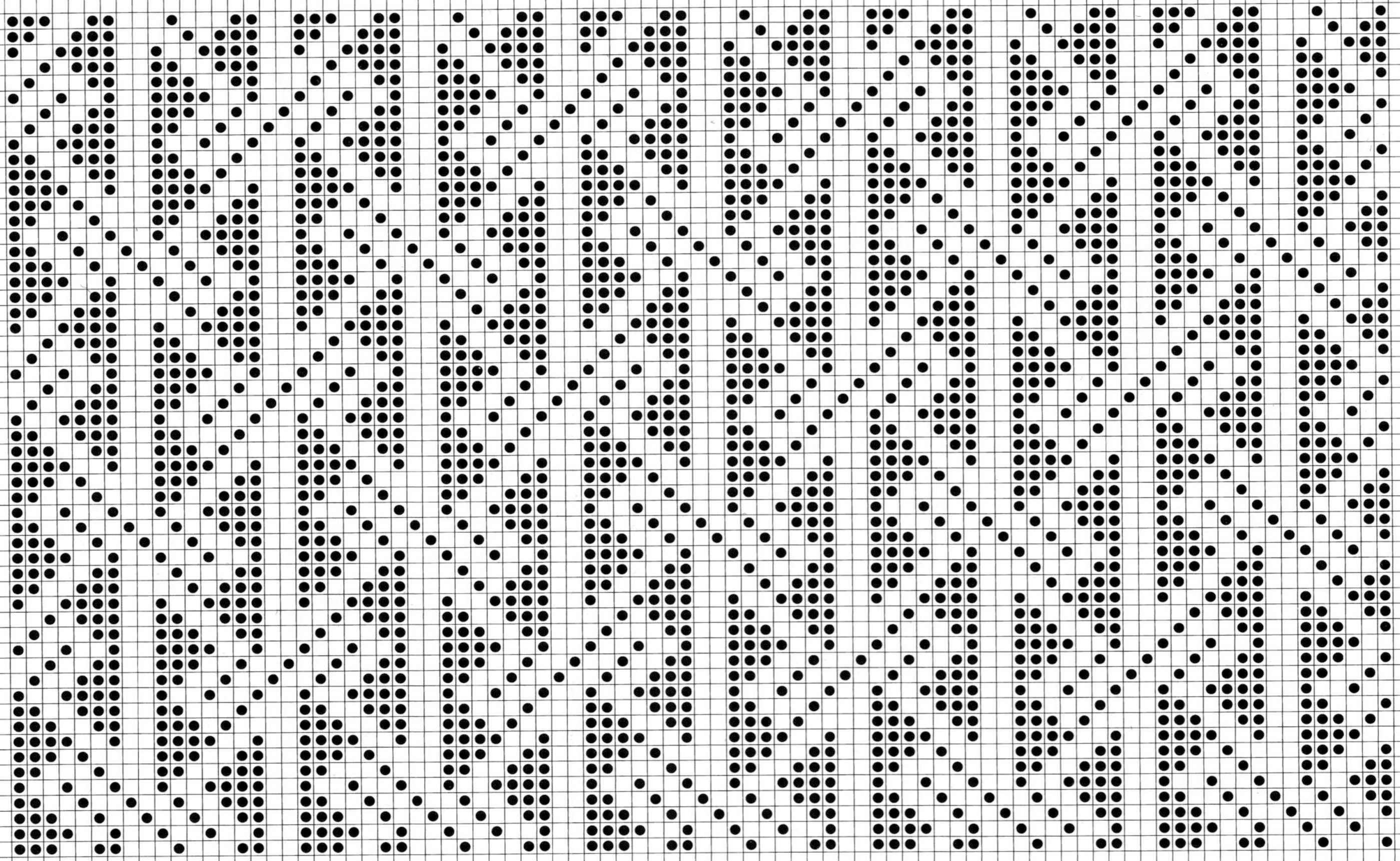

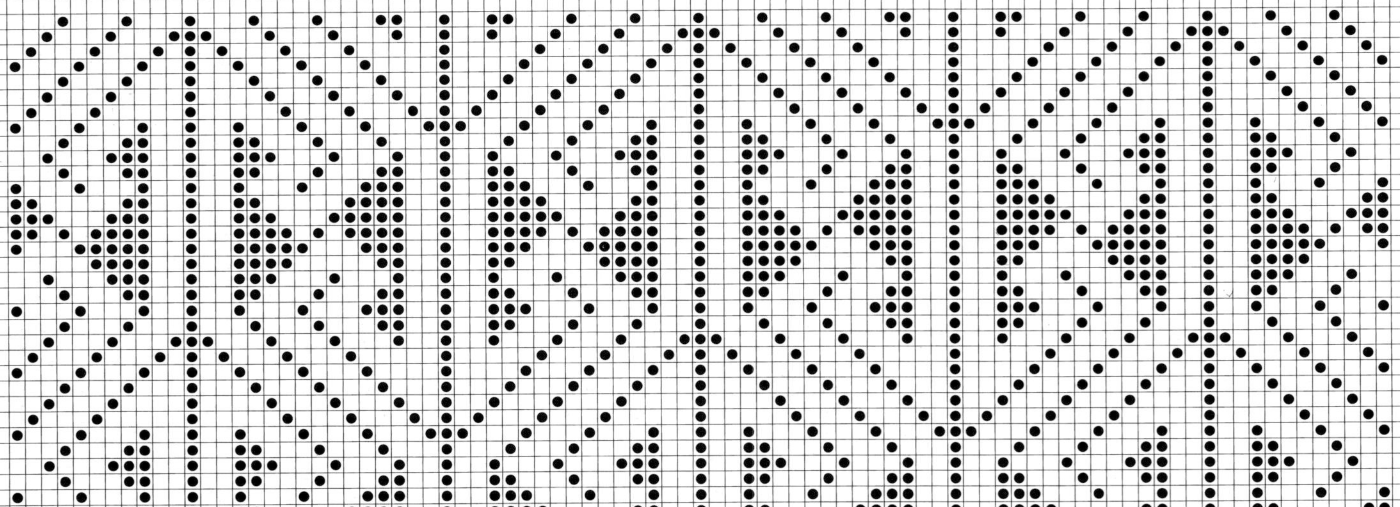

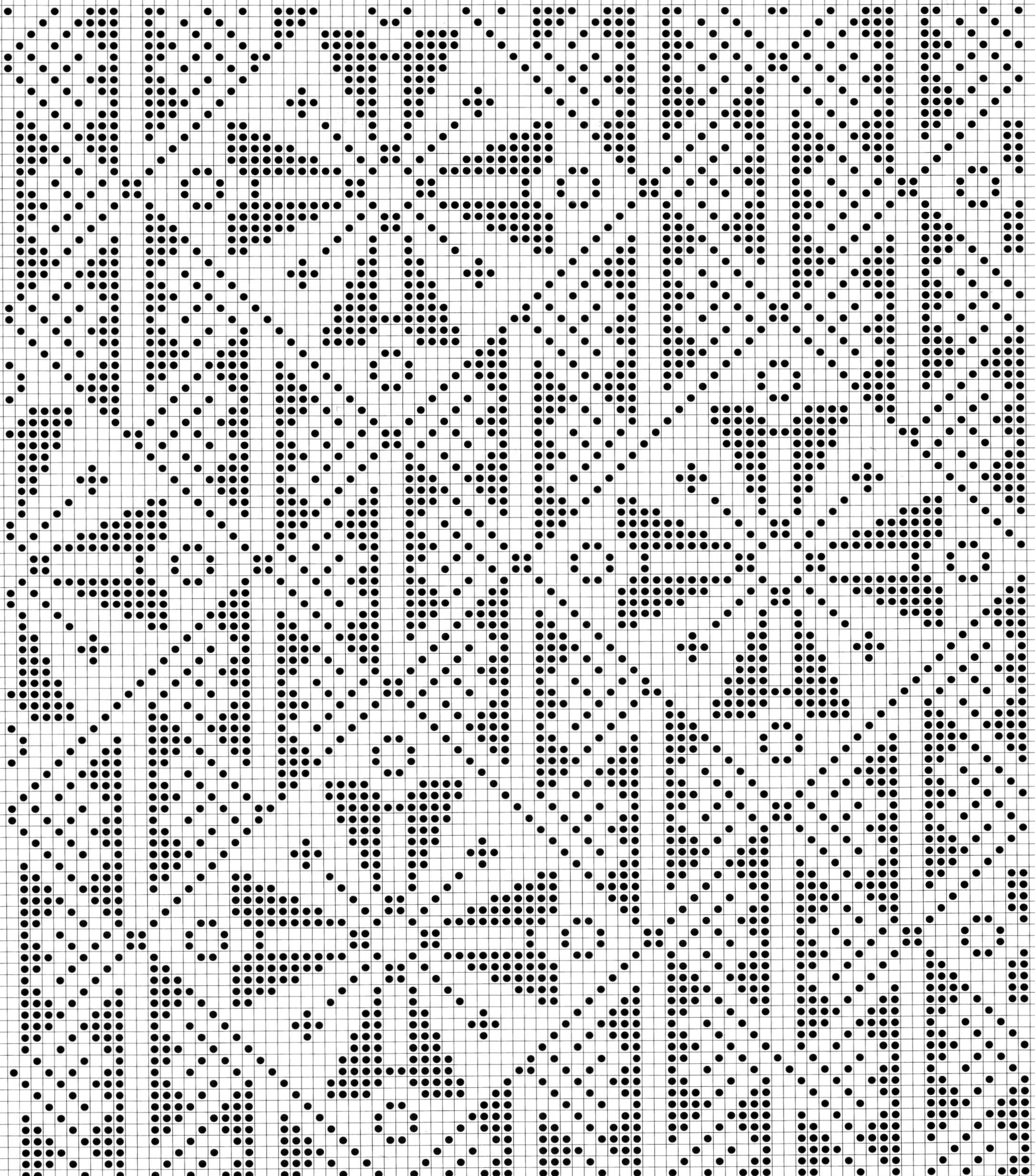

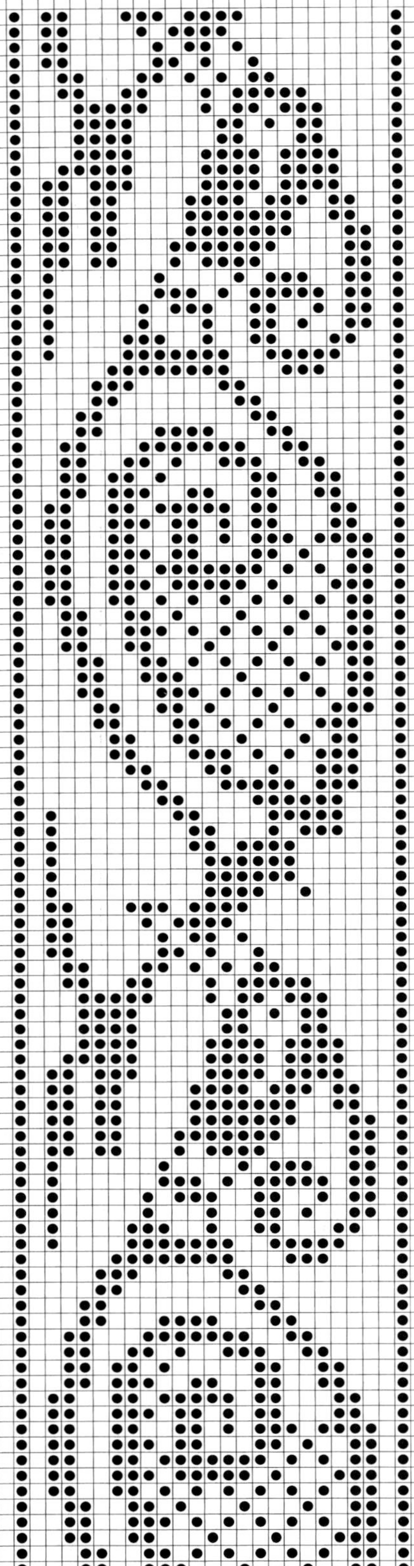

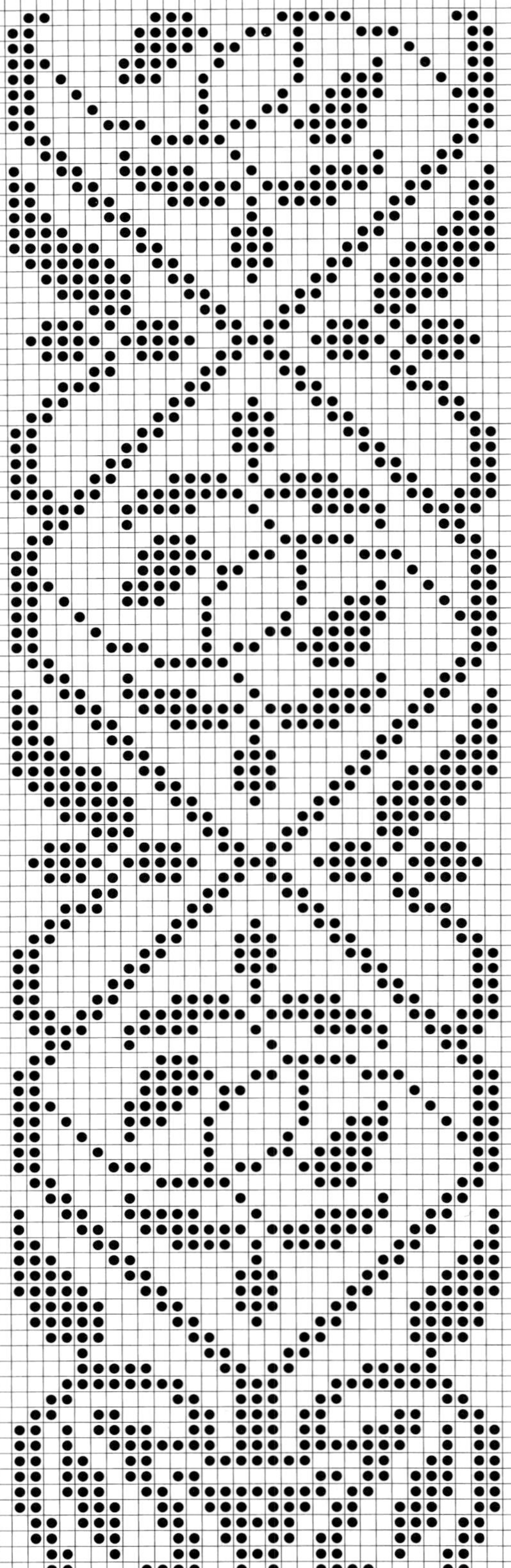

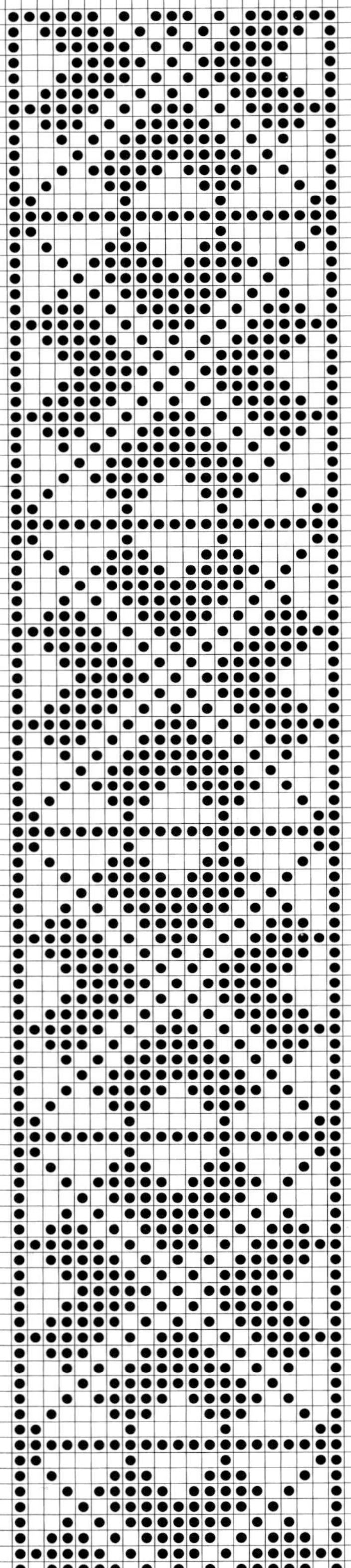

GREECE

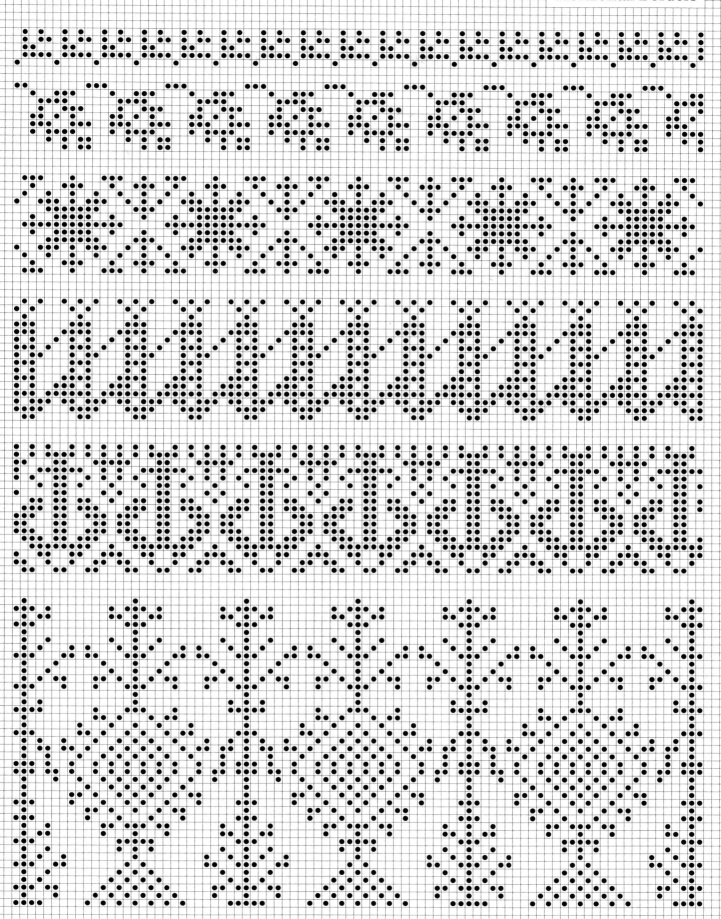

THE
CAUCASUS

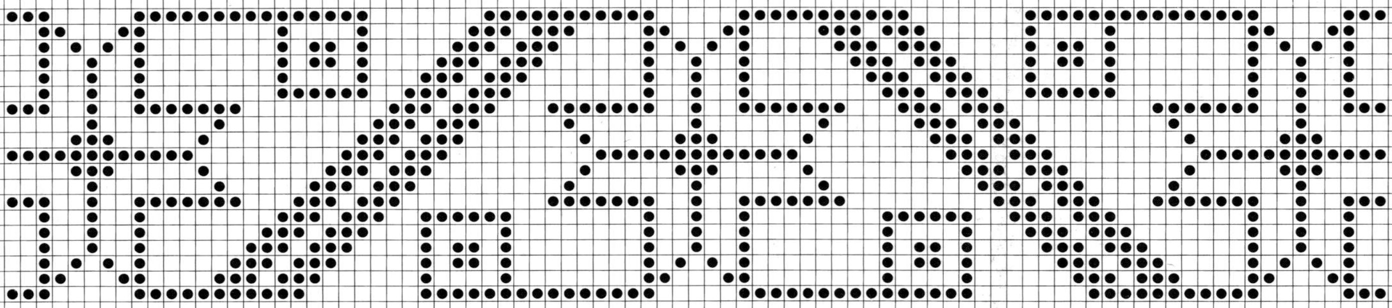

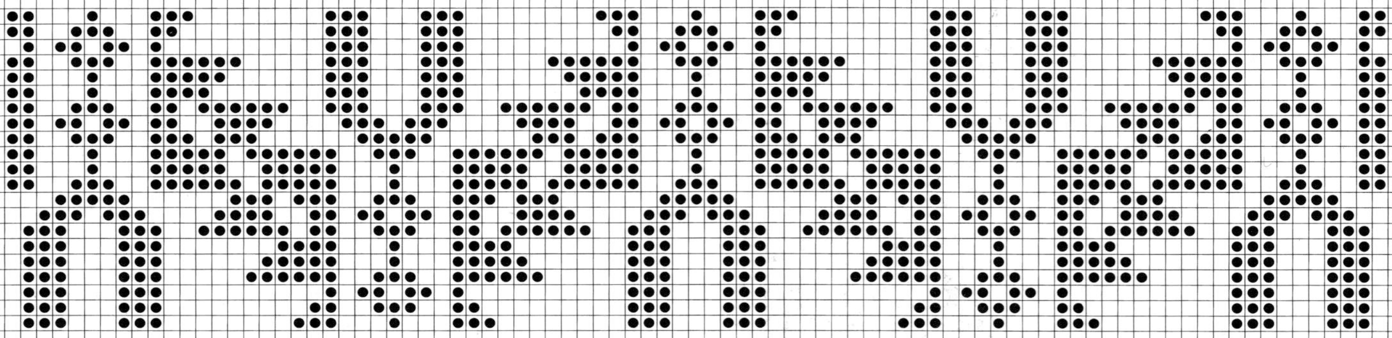

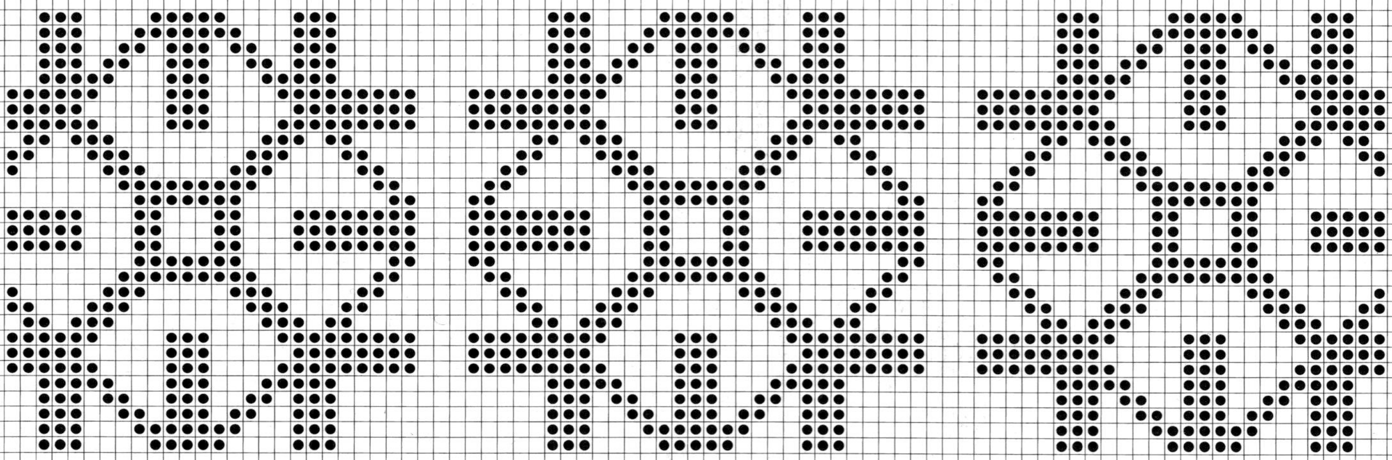

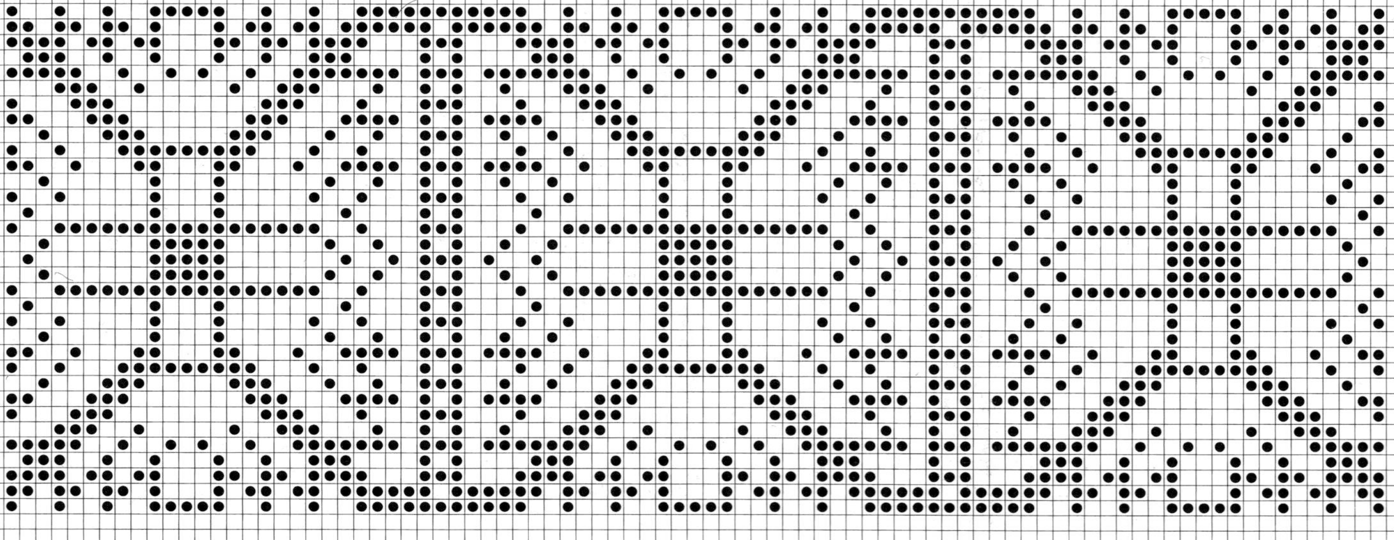

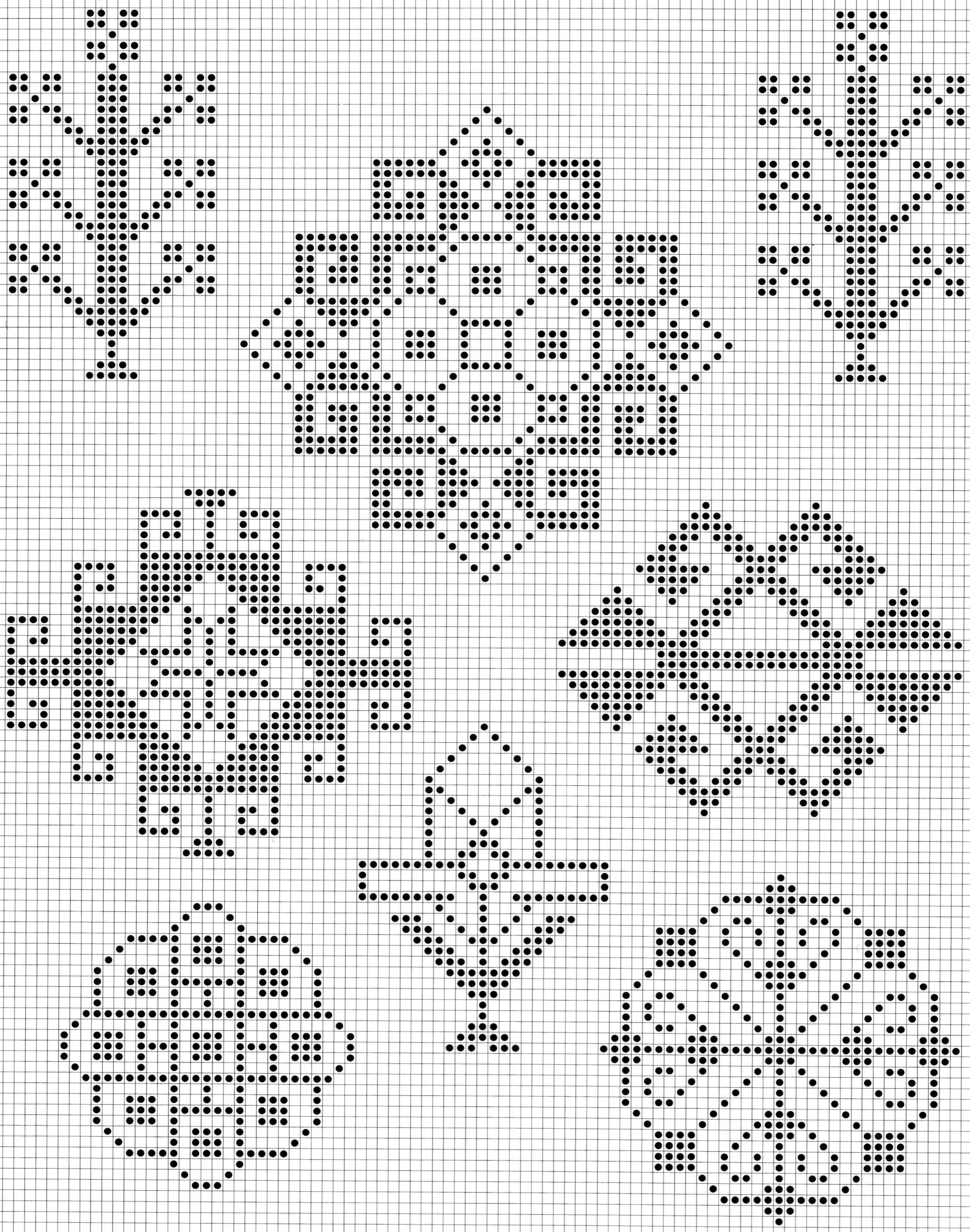

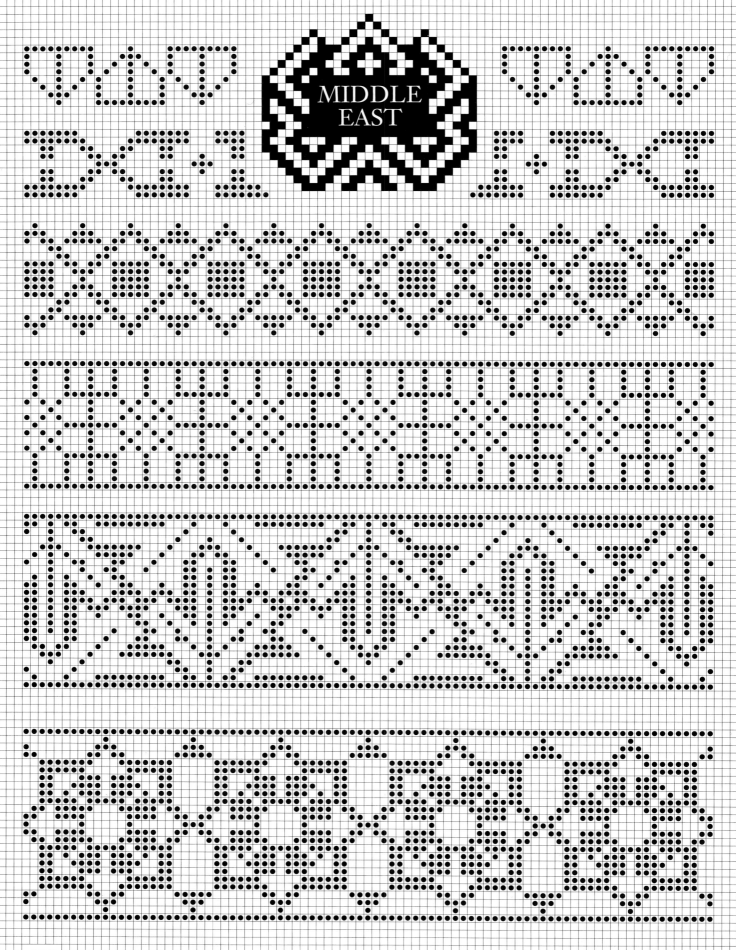

MIDDLE EAST

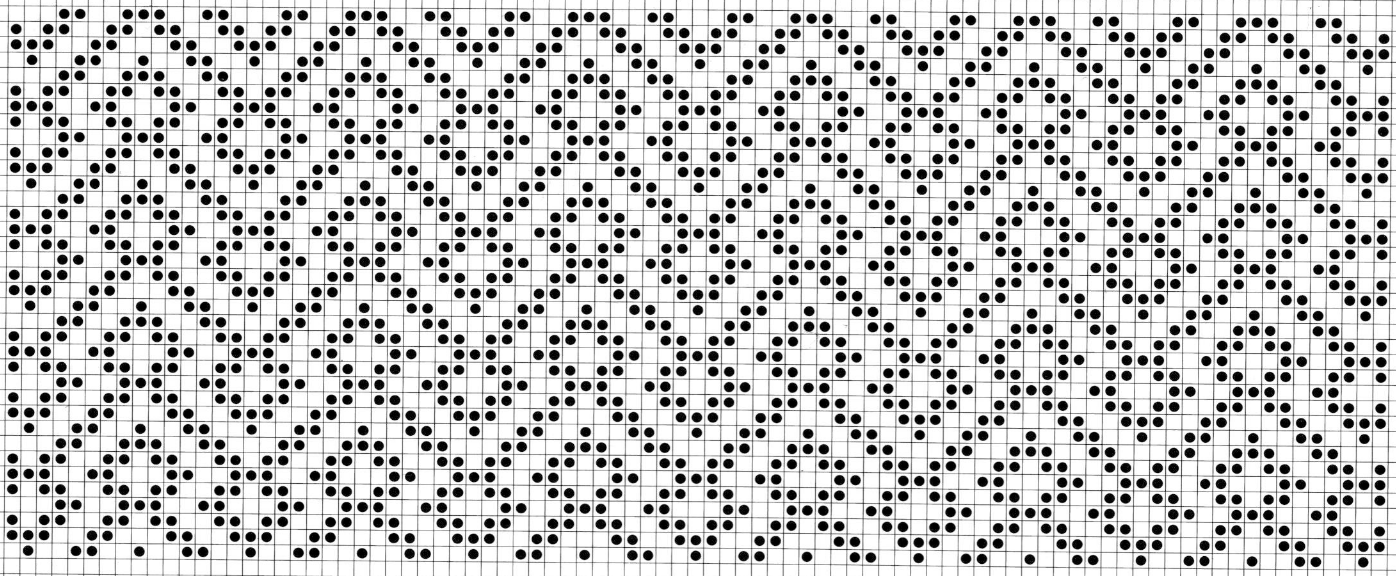

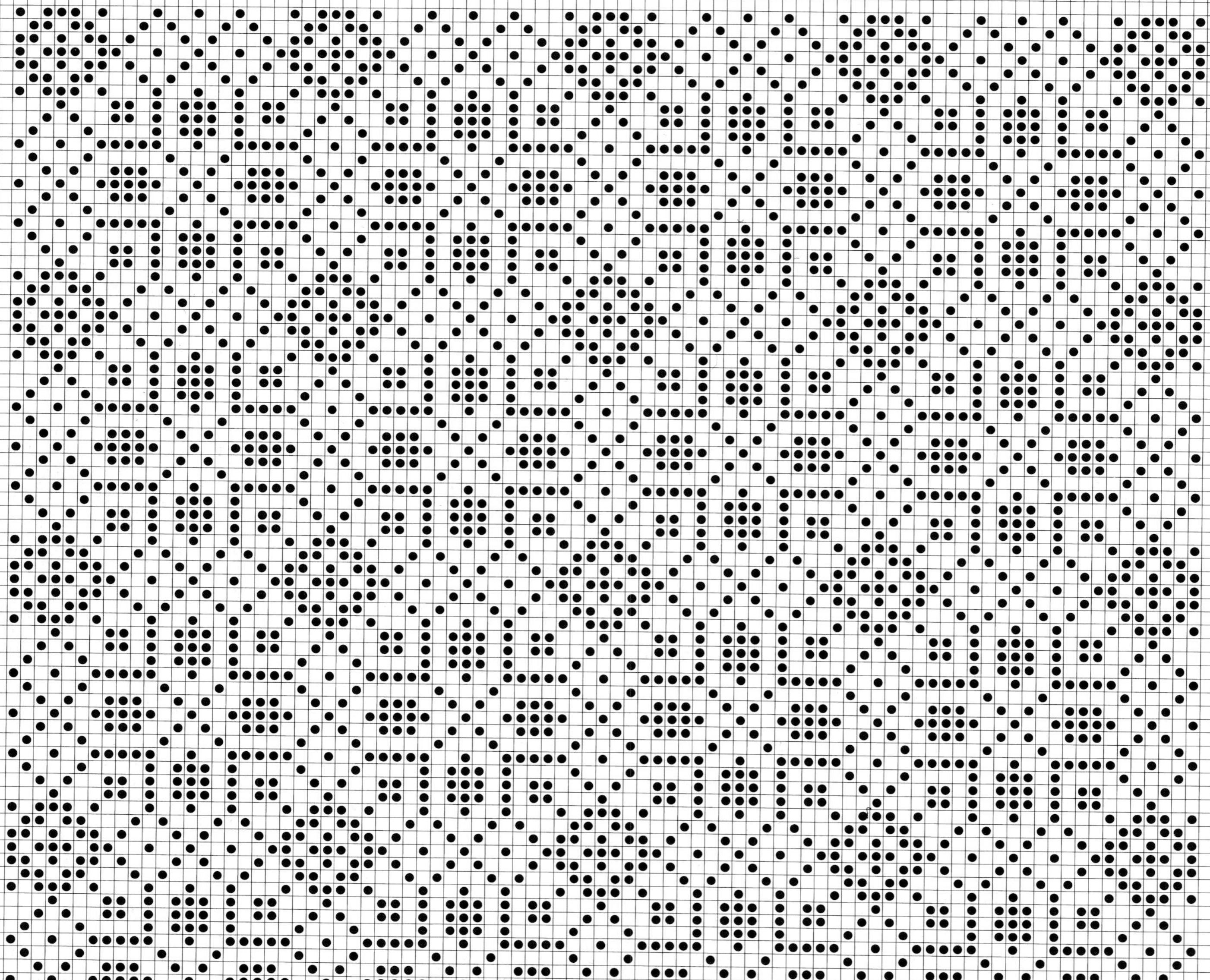

FAR
EAST

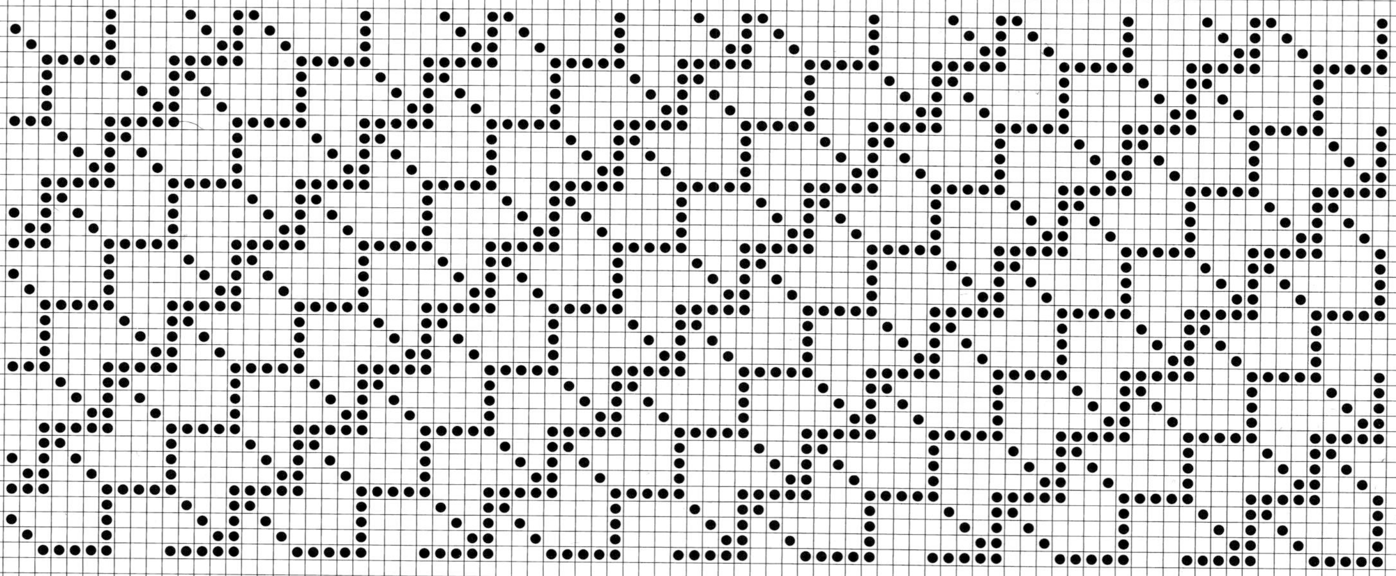

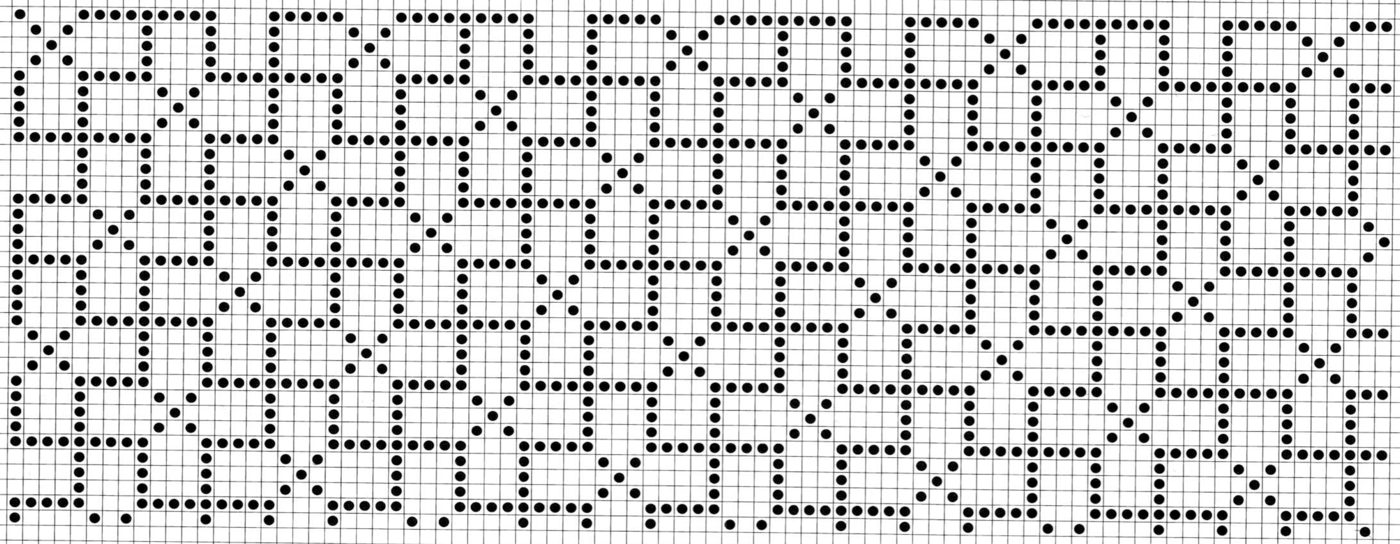

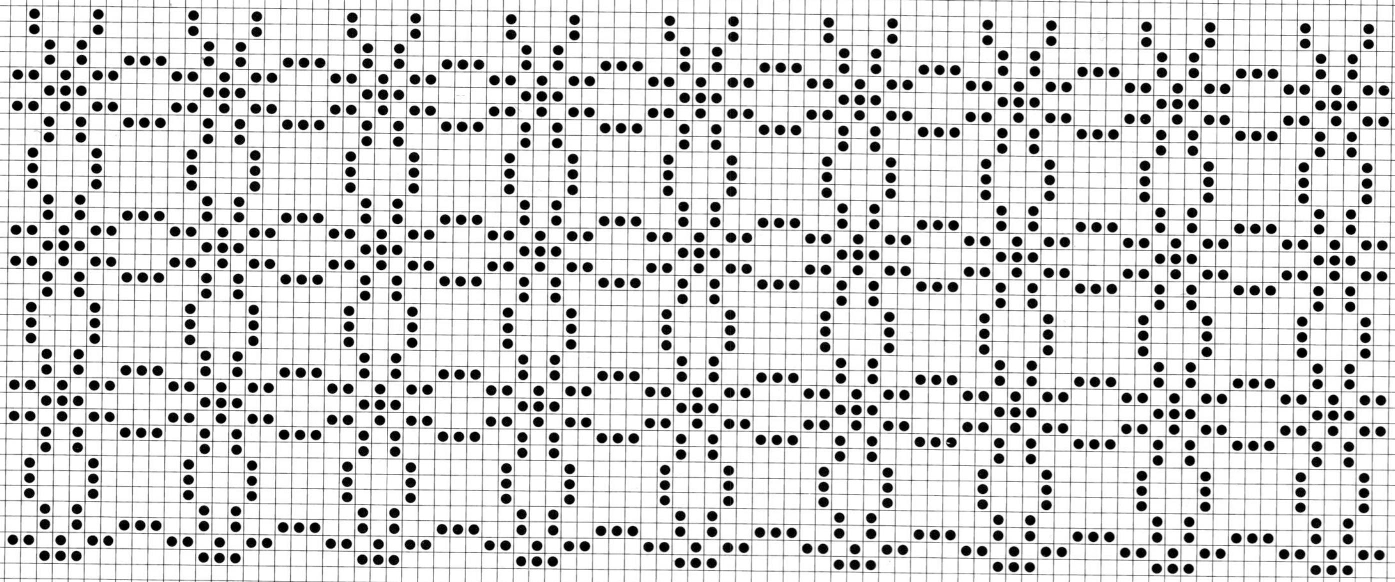

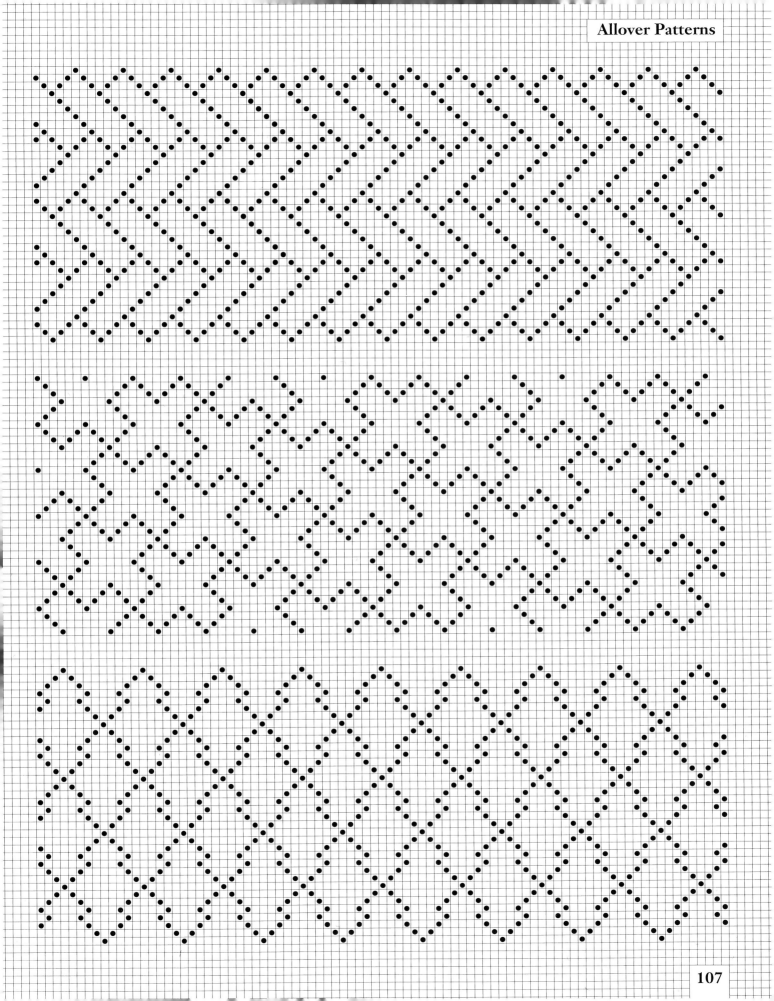

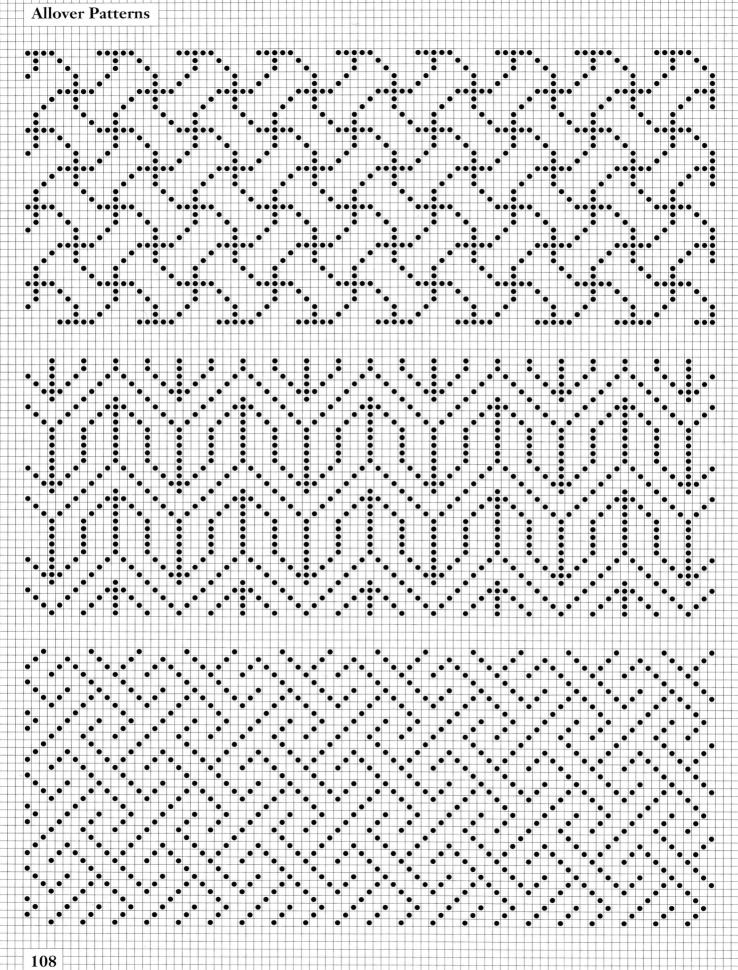

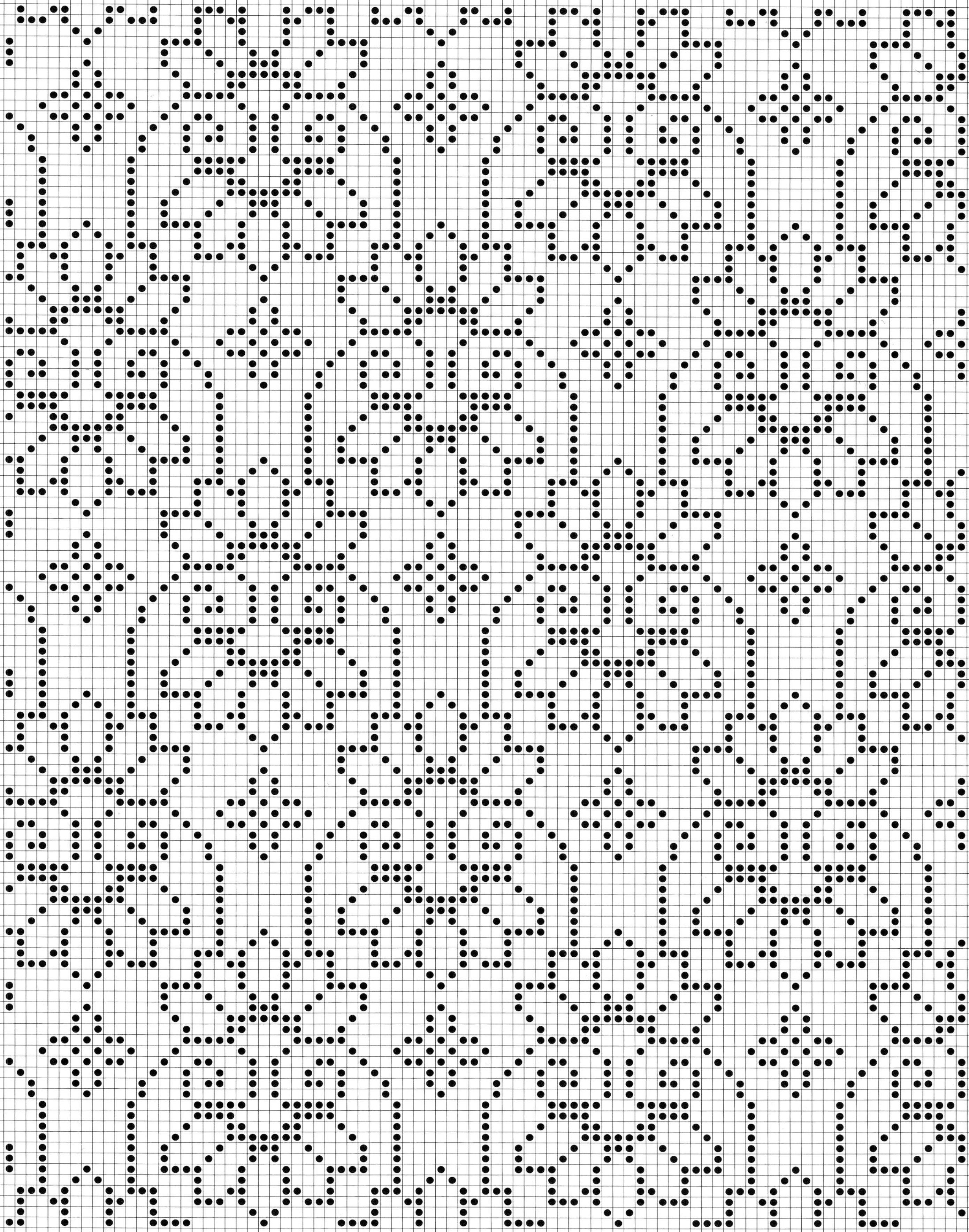

The Continuing Story

My pattern library is constantly being extended with patterns I have constructed myself. Creating new patterns is at the heart of my design work and this chapter illustrates that continuing story. When time and circumstance permit, I find it relaxing and pleasurable to sit with a blank sheet of graph paper and a sharpened pencil, and let the imagination run. Nature is my most consistent source of inspiration, for in between travels, I live on a Hebridean island dominated by moorland, sea and shoreline—and many of the following patterns reflect this fact.

A pattern may be the result of a walk across the moor or along a beach—or a trip to New York. Sometimes it will arise from a specific design project. The thistles on pages 120 and 121 are the result of a quest for a design with an emblematic Scottish theme. Other patterns have stemmed from a journey through the *Inner Landscape* of abstract geometry. They start with a single dot upon the page, which travels in whatever direction the mind takes.

How does a body of traditional patterns begin, and is it ever complete? The tradition must begin with an idea—either copied or original—and a sense of experiment. In my opinion, it will only be complete when every knitter has lost the urge to take it further, for the story is not finished—and I hope it never will be.

Right: A playful arrangement of some of my Sea & Shoreline designs, worked in bright and breezy colours of Alice Starmore® *Hebridean 2 Ply*.

BIRDS & FLOWERS

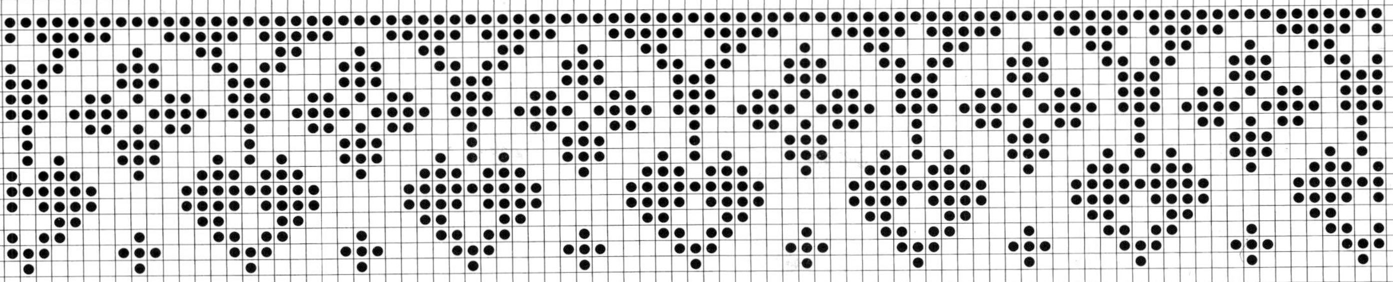

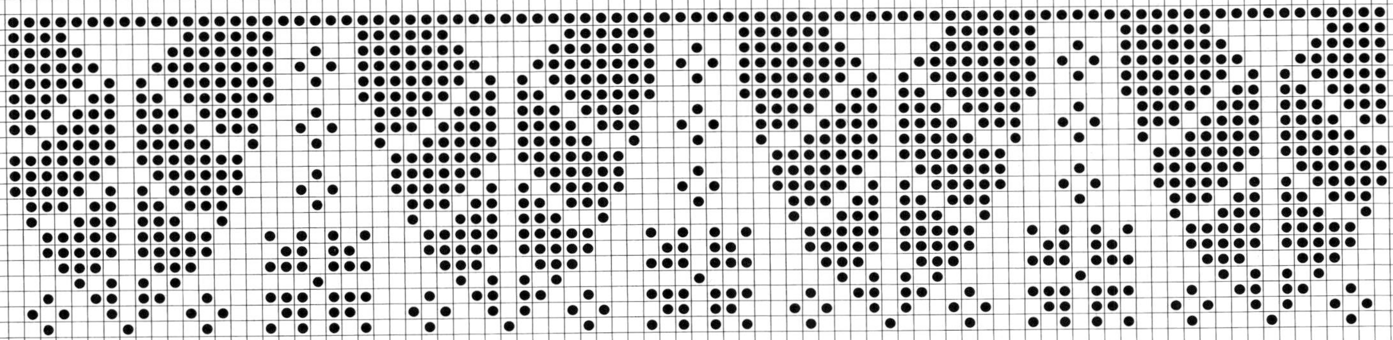

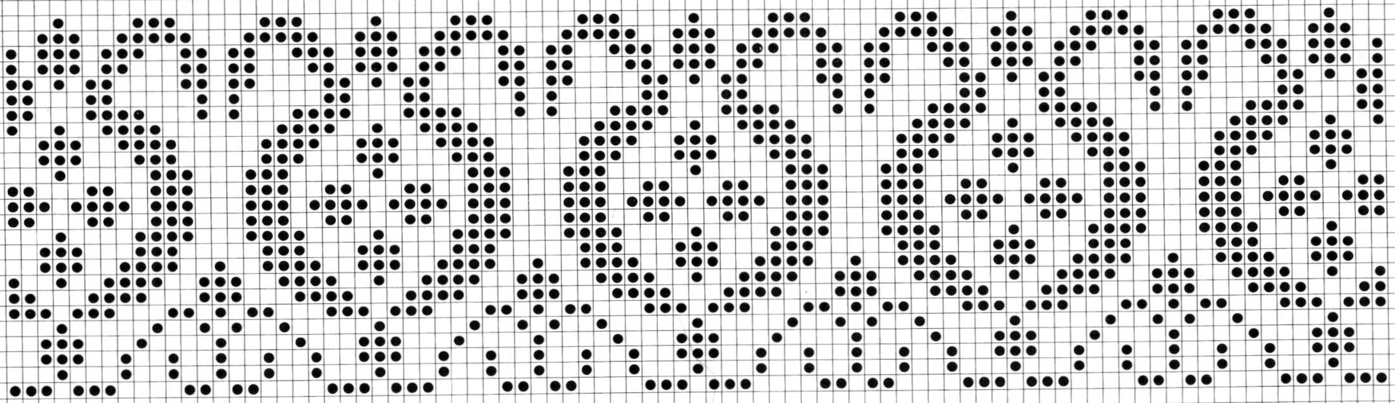

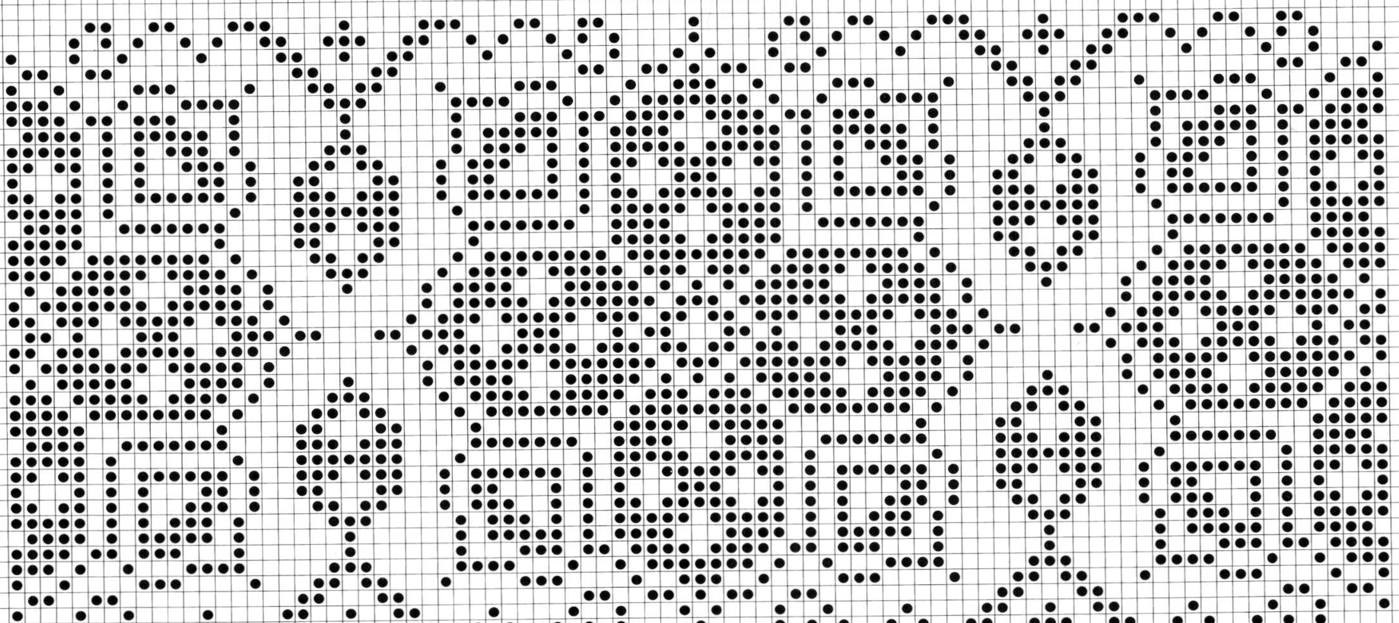

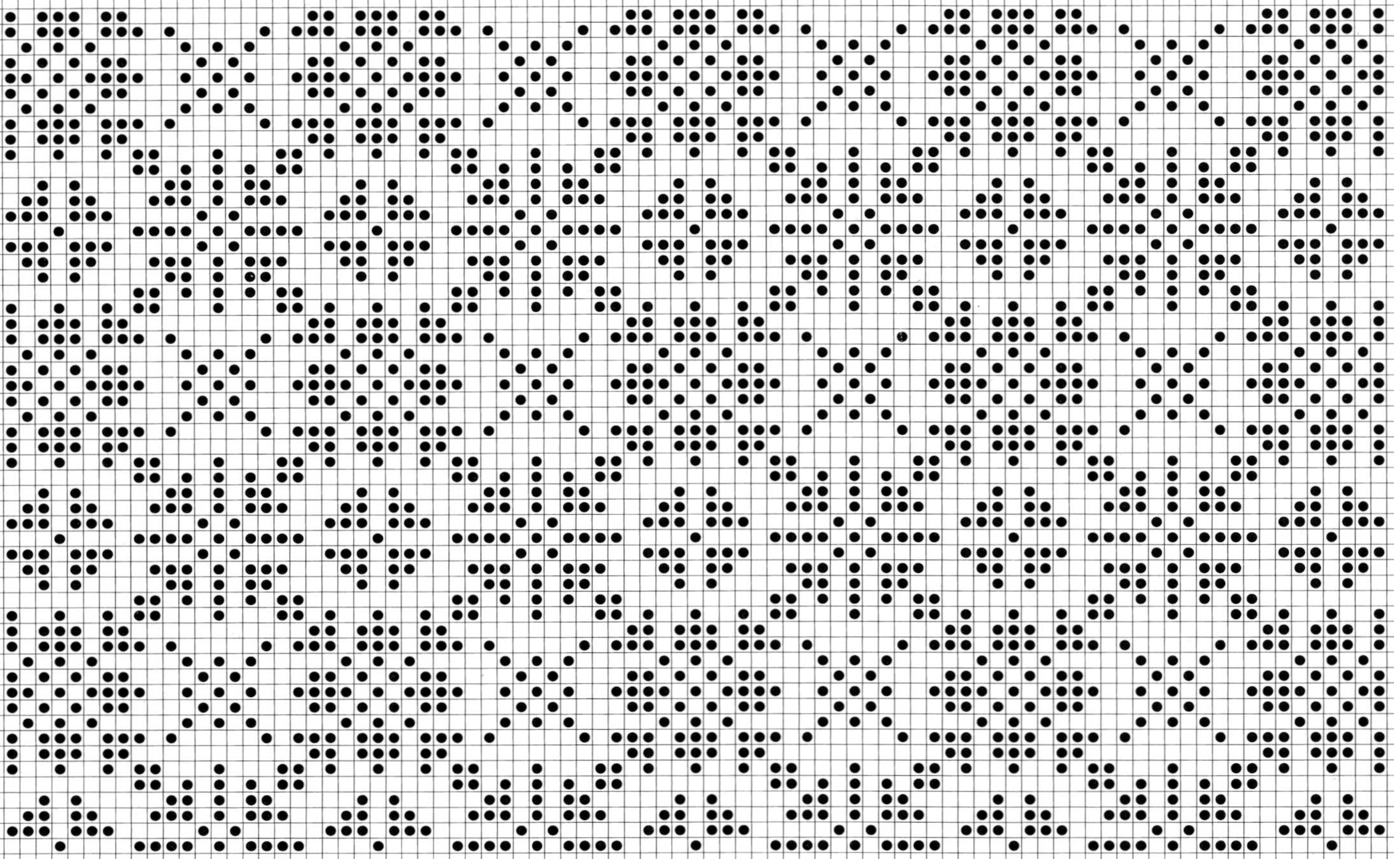

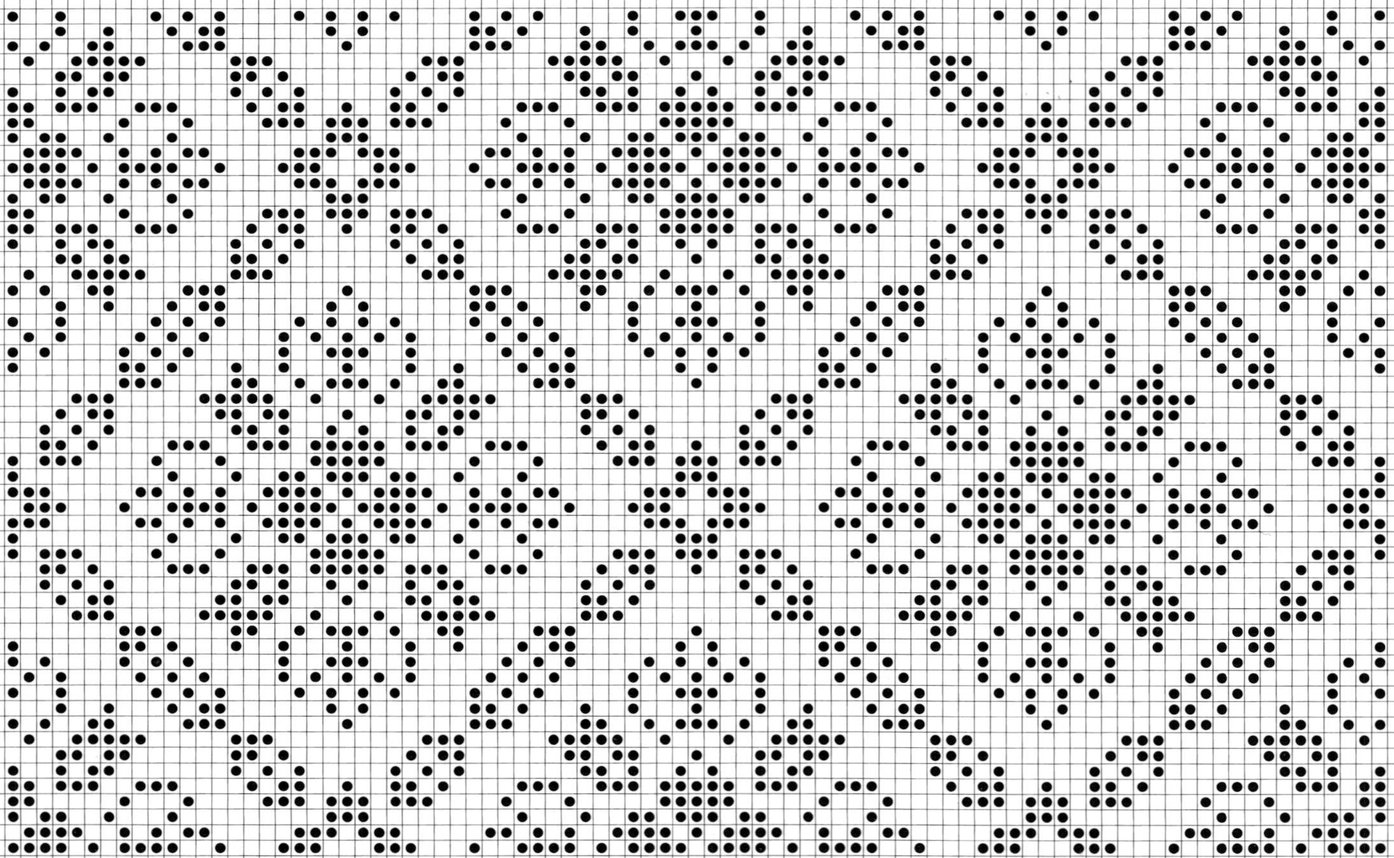

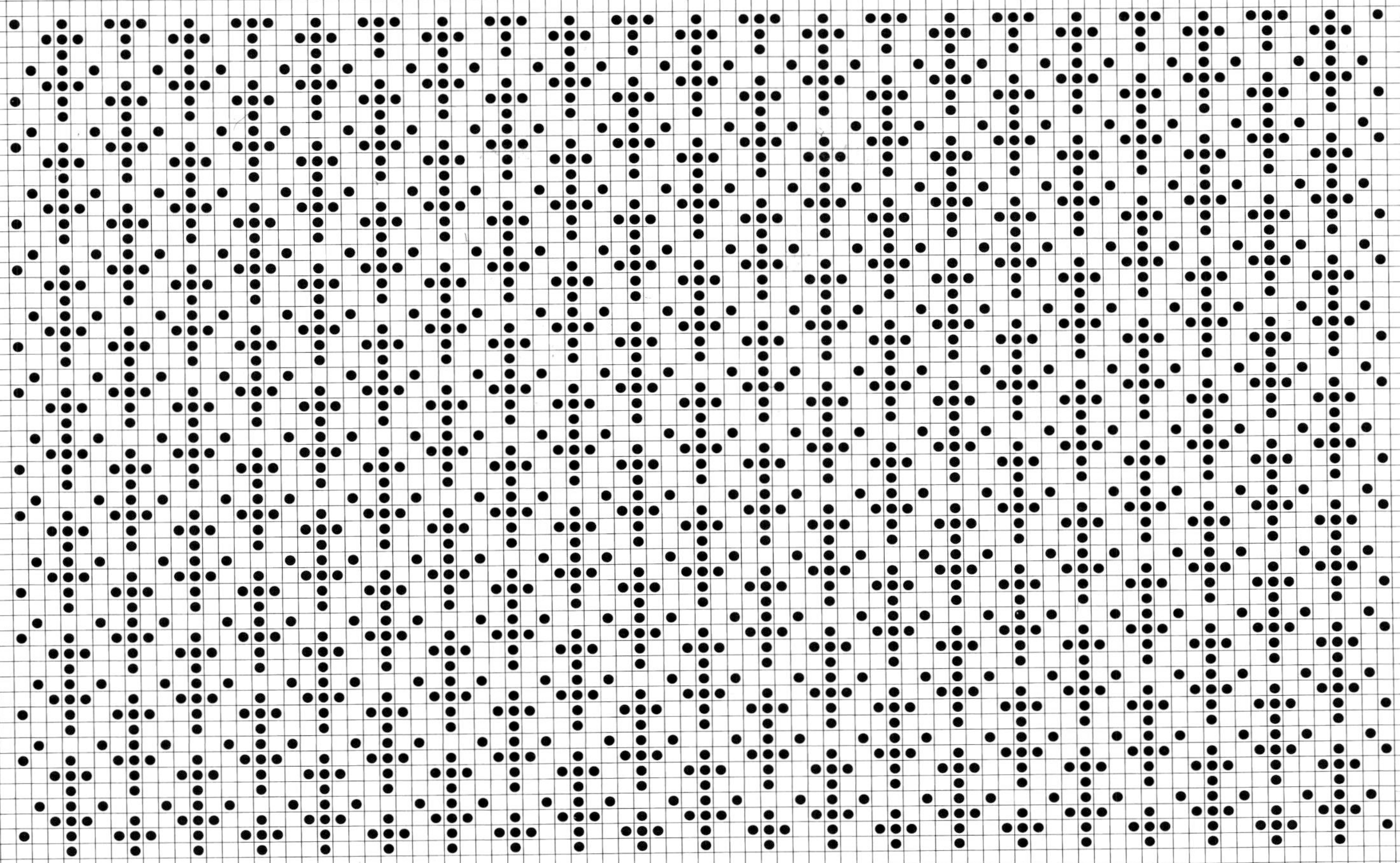

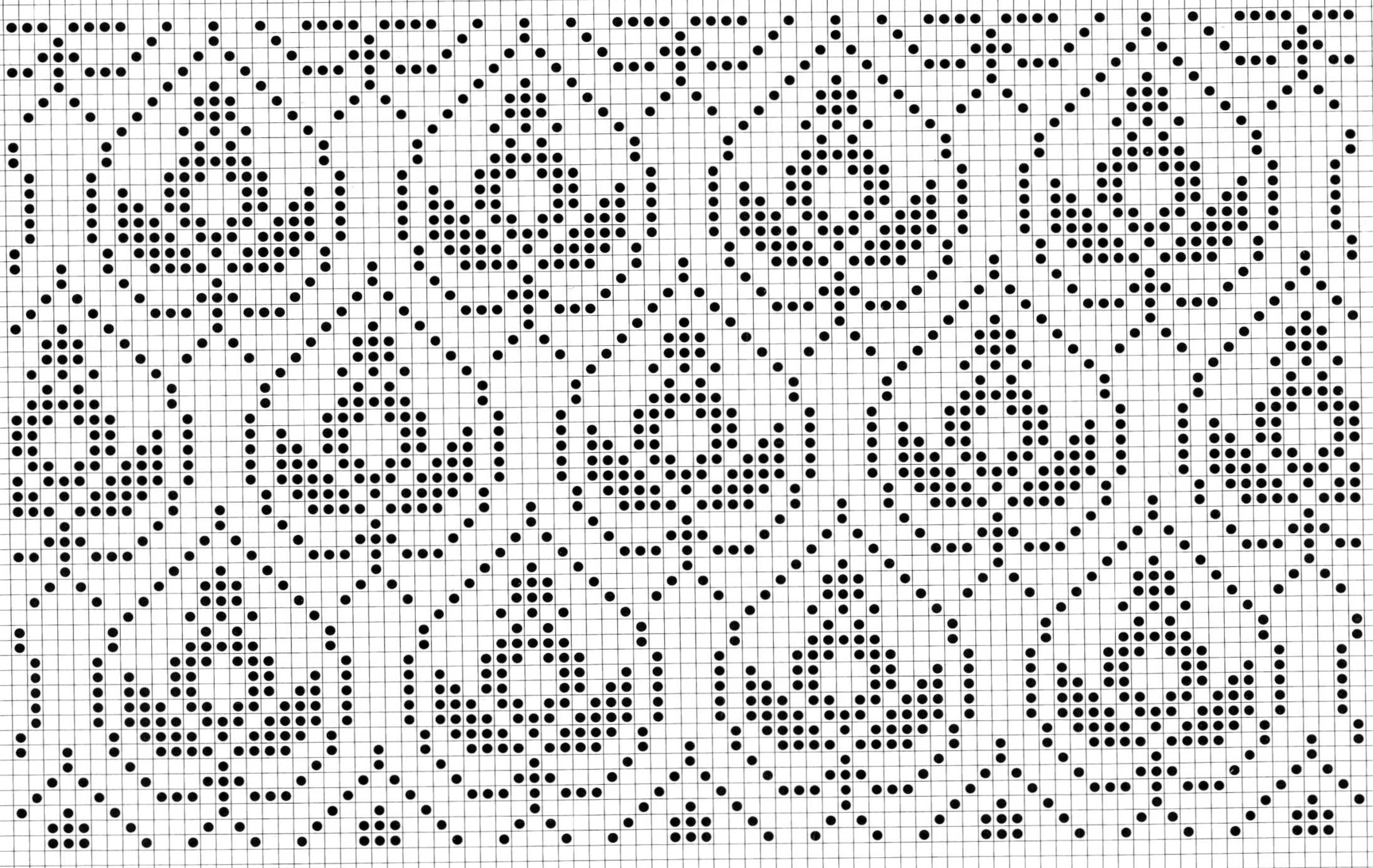

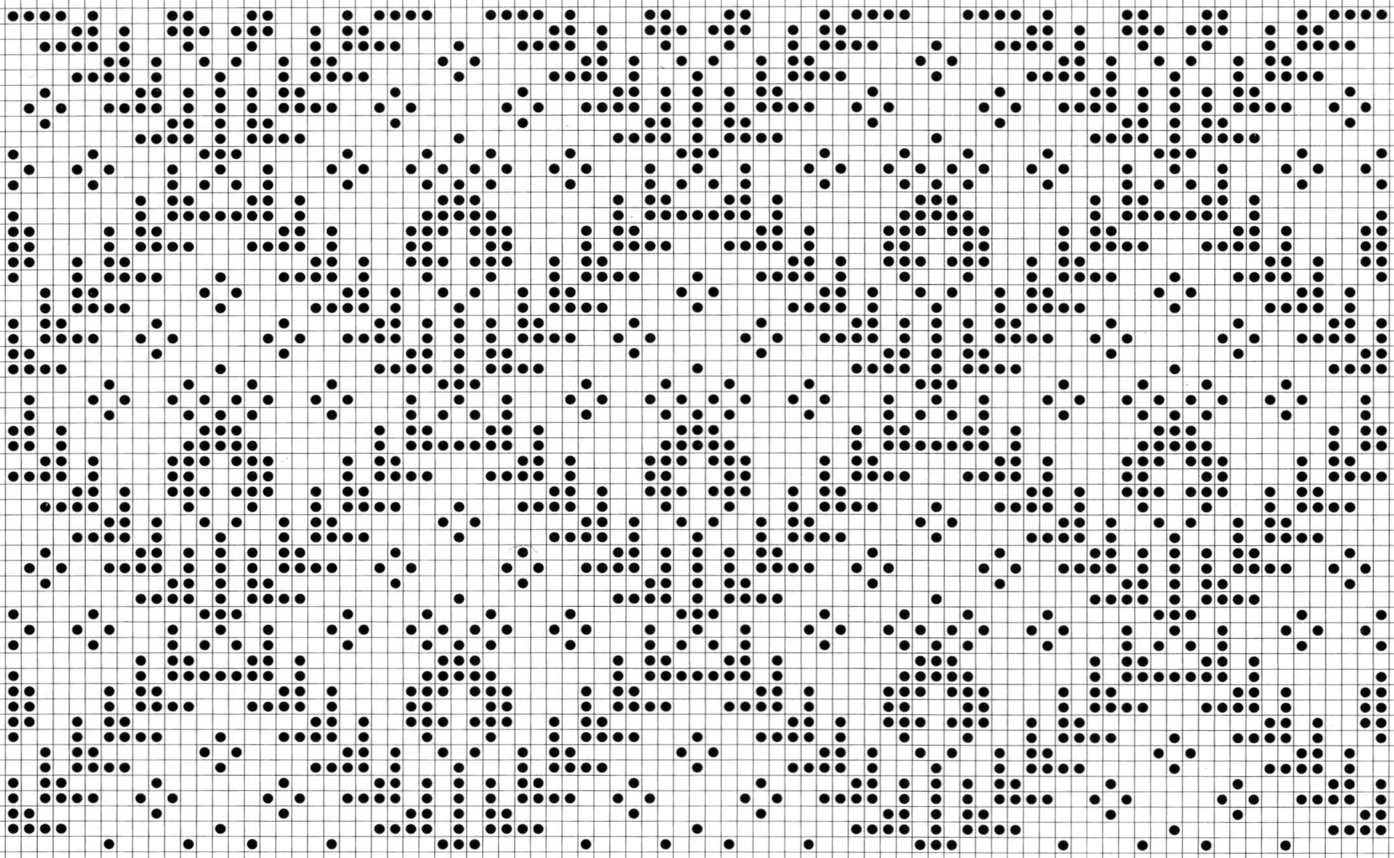

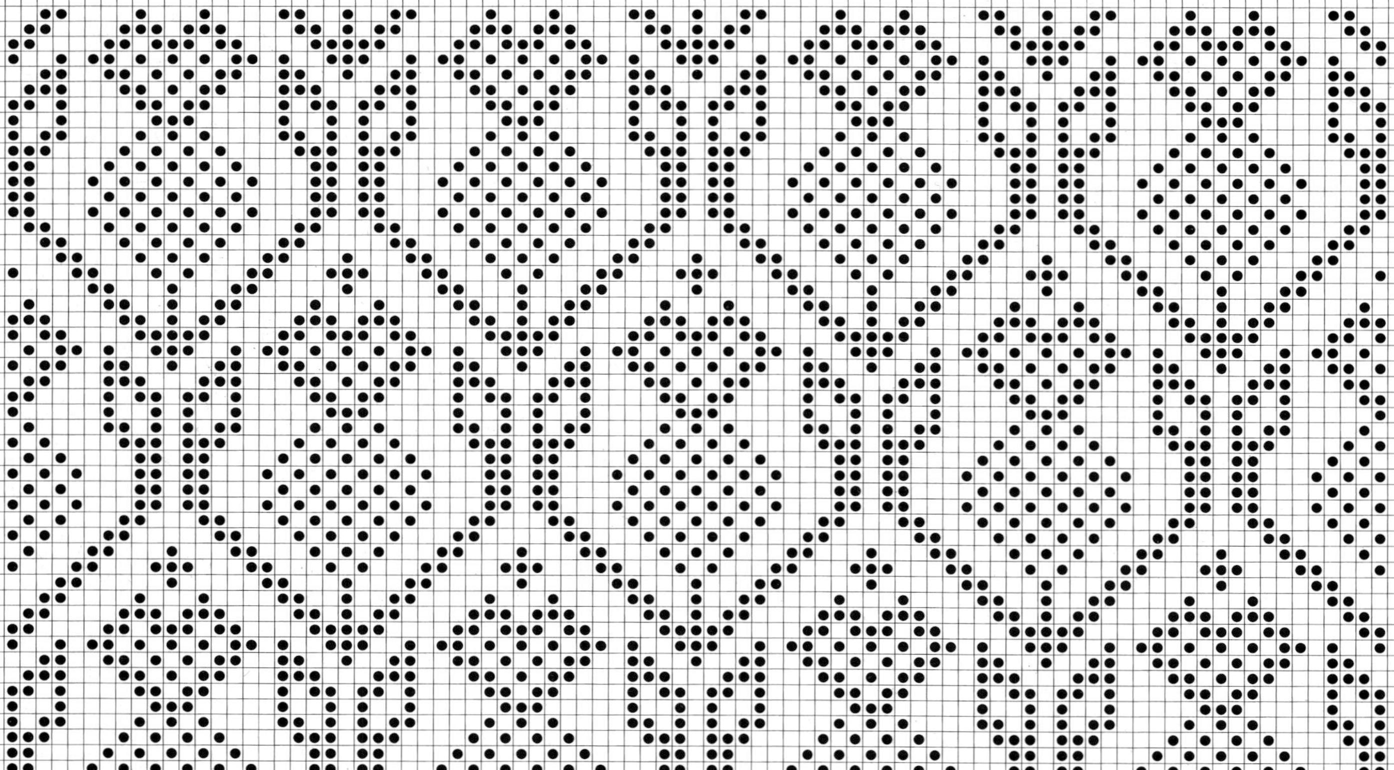

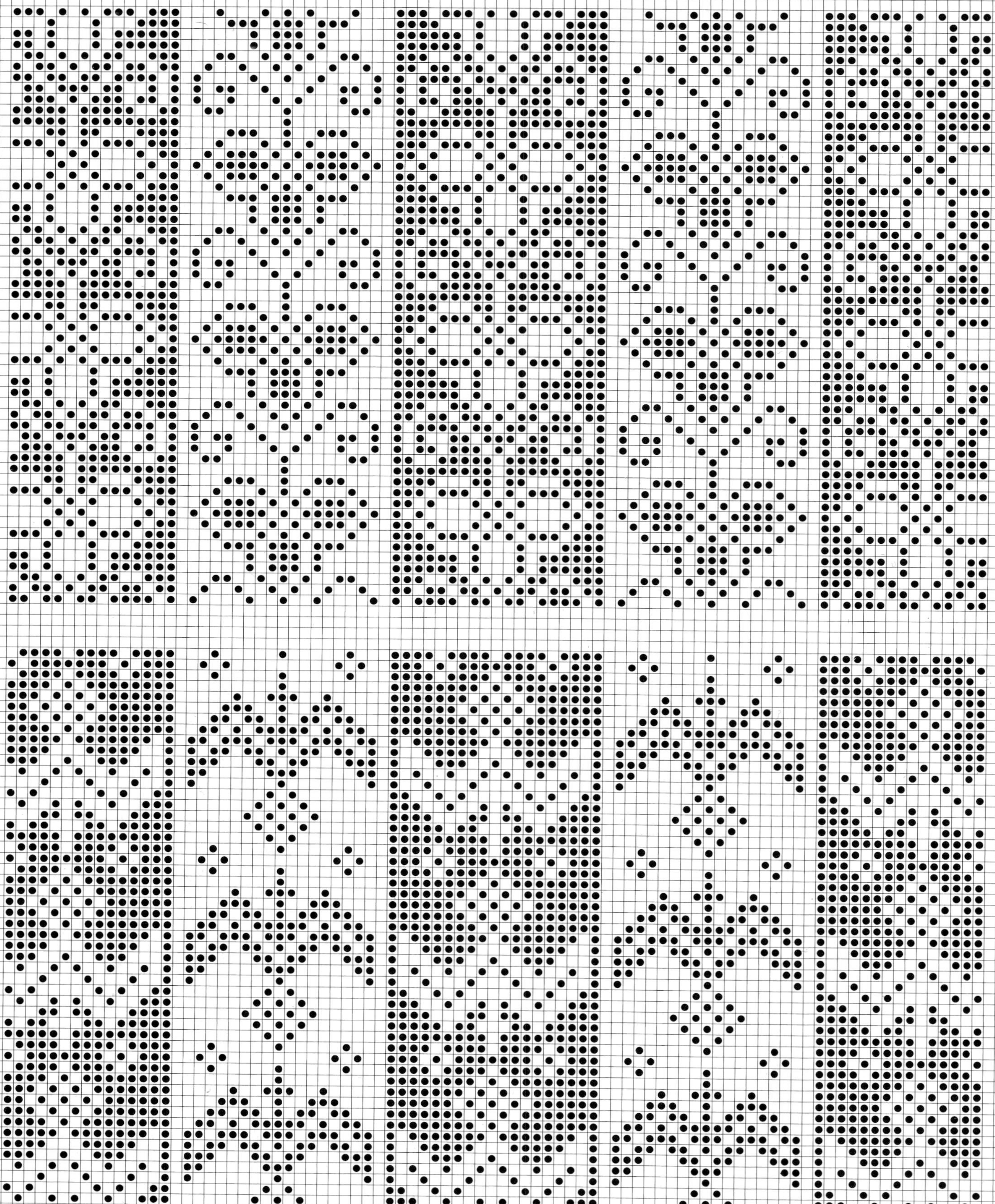

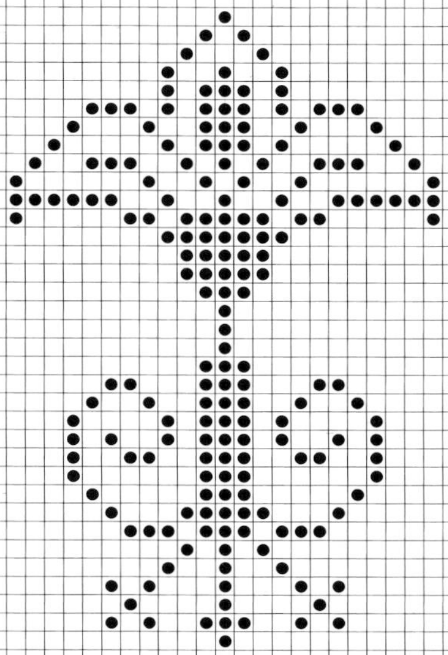

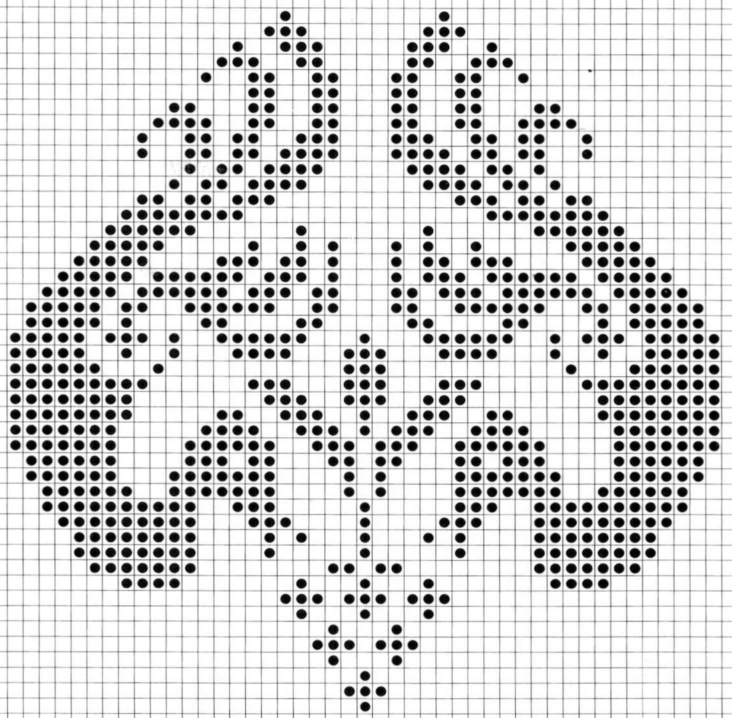

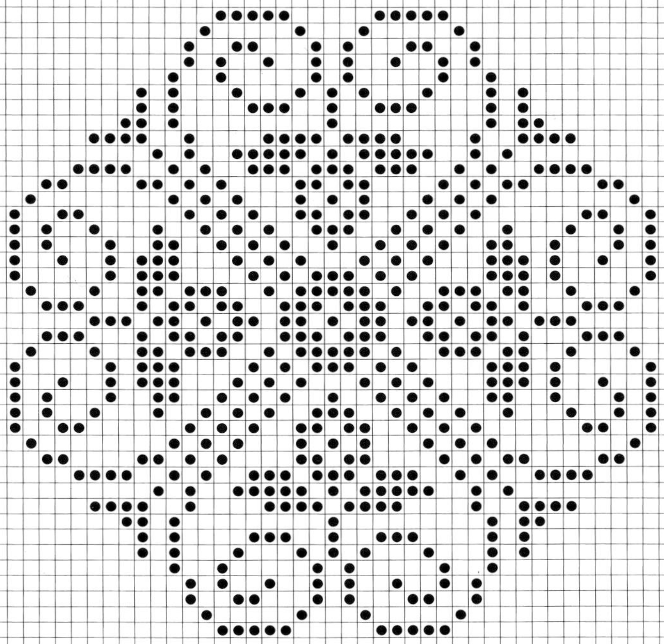

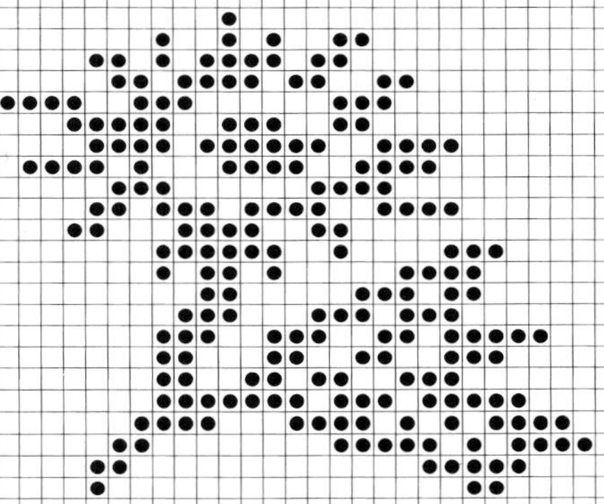

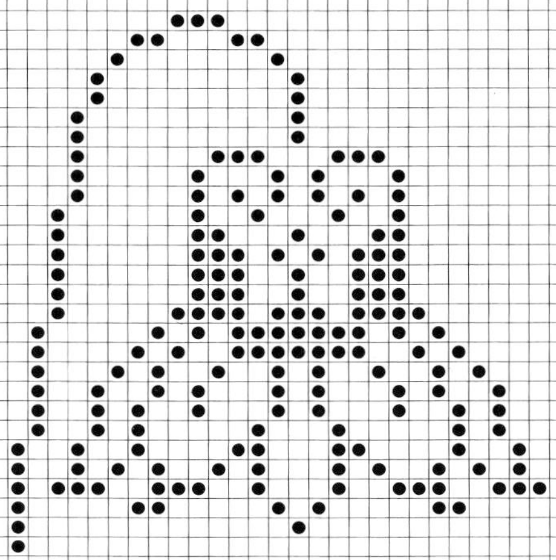

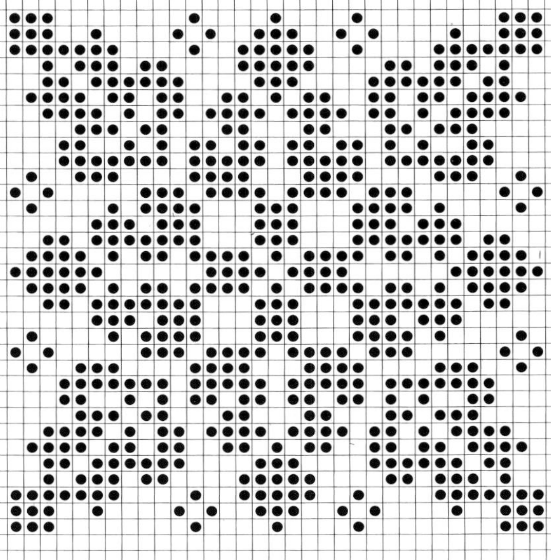

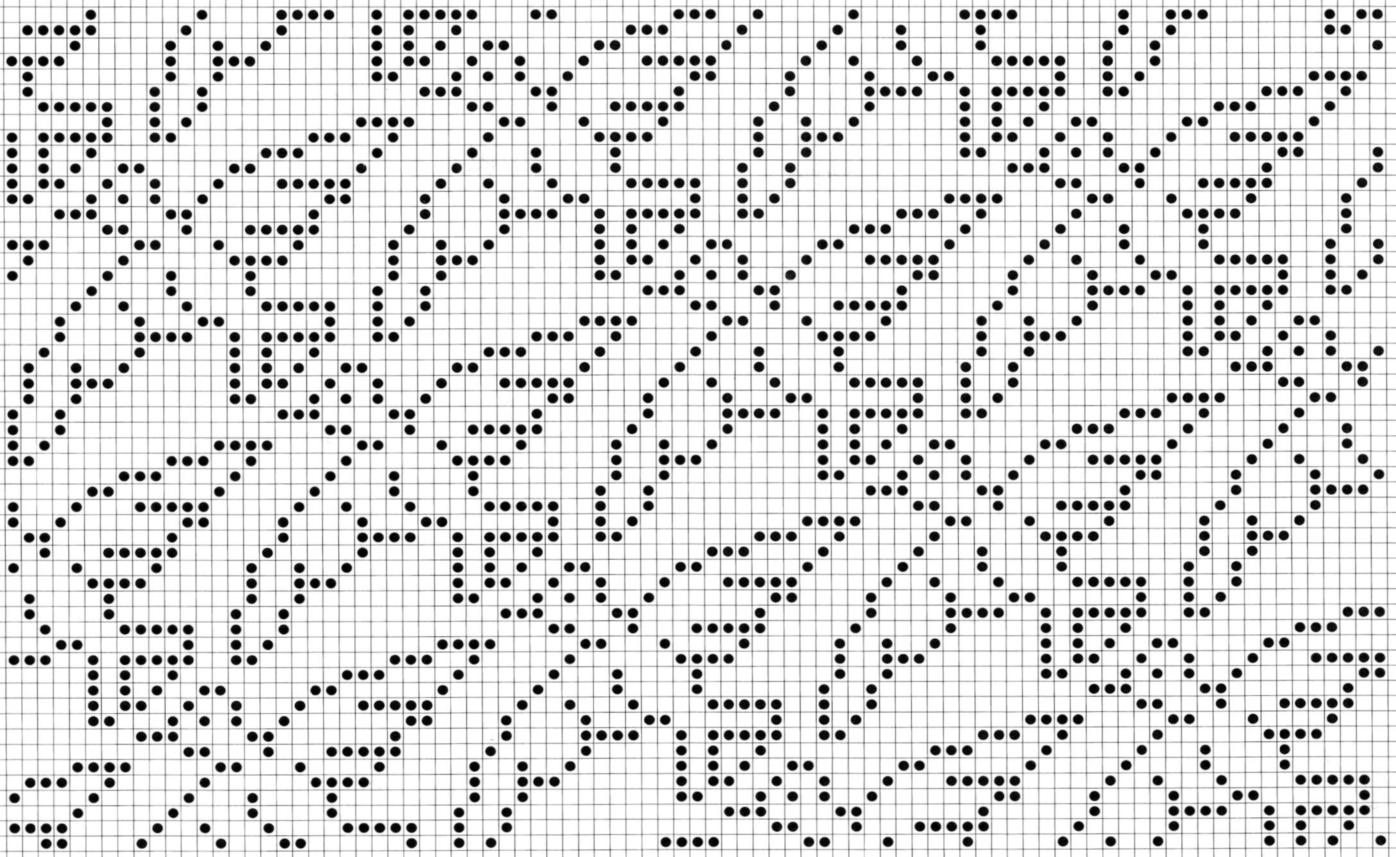

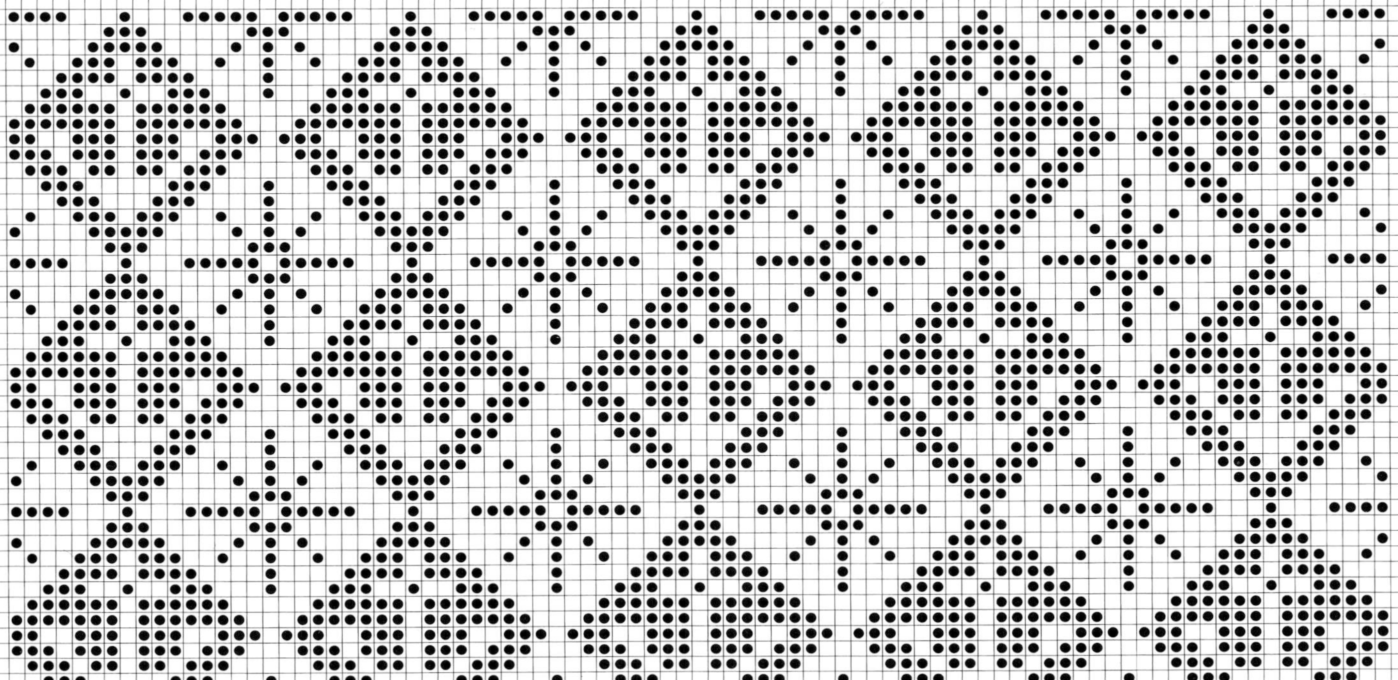

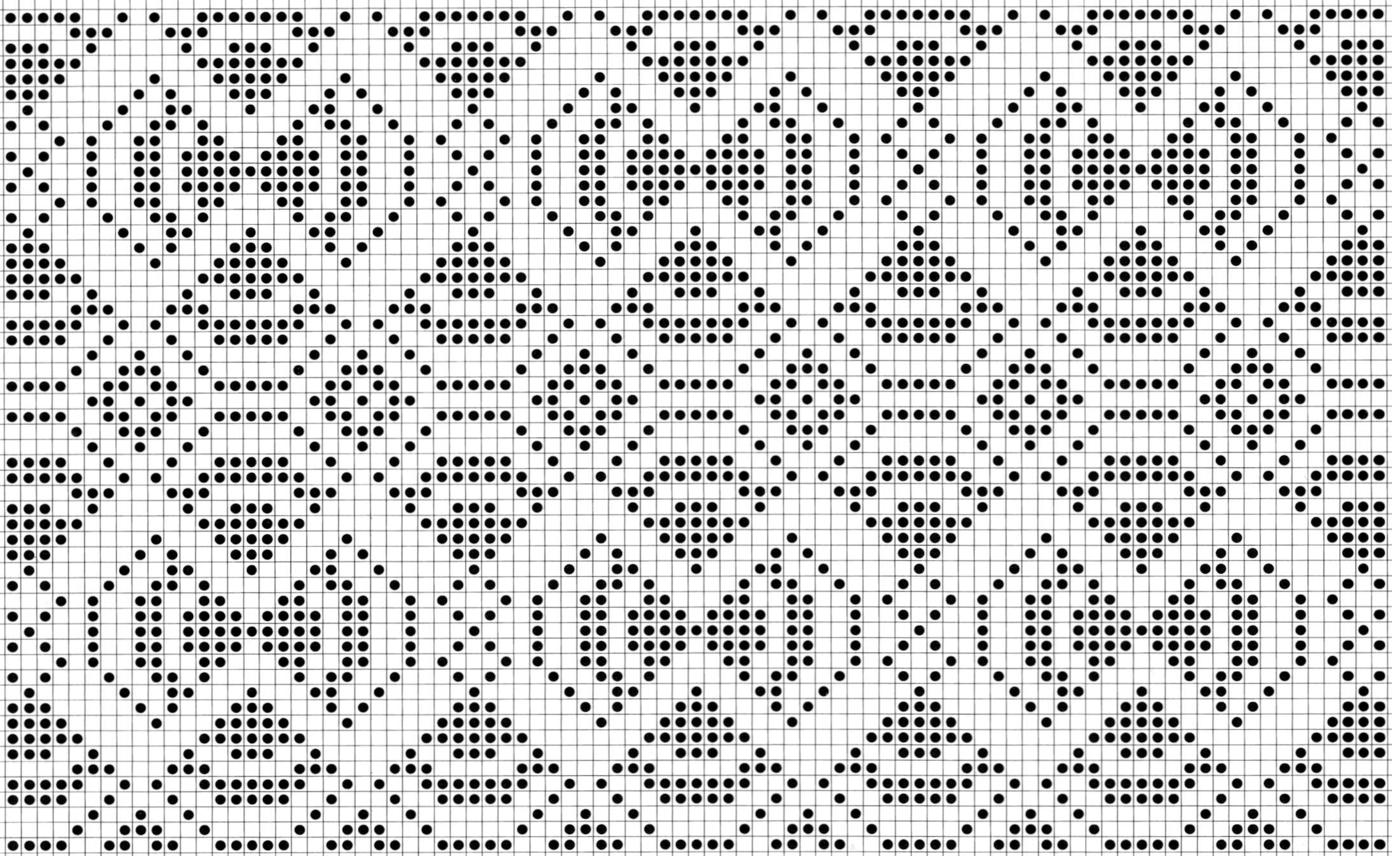

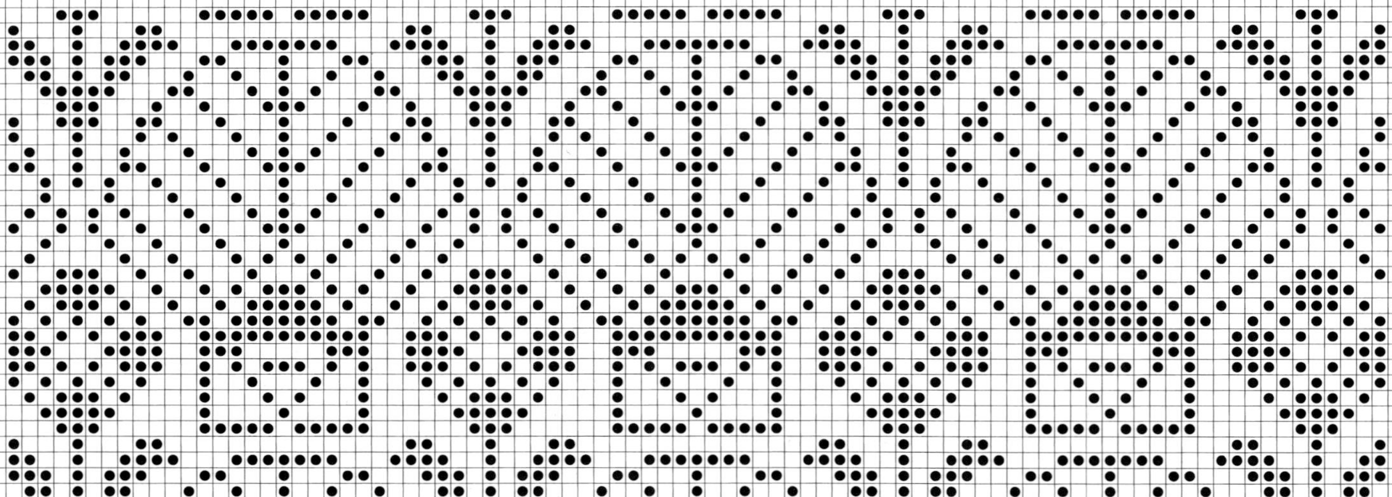

THE
INNER
LANDSCAPE

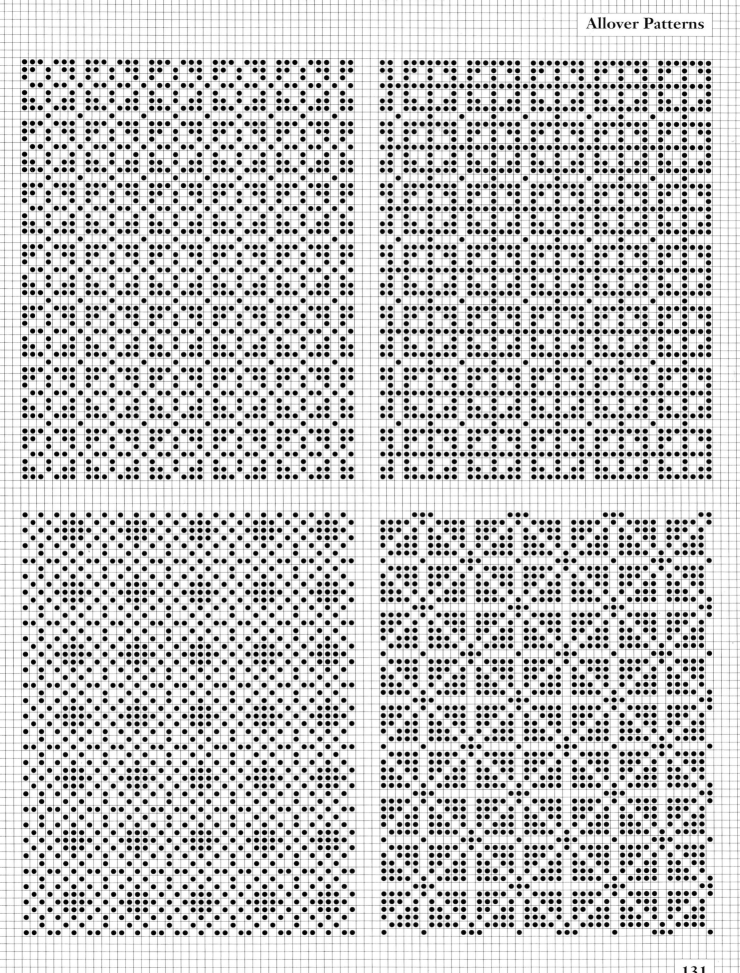

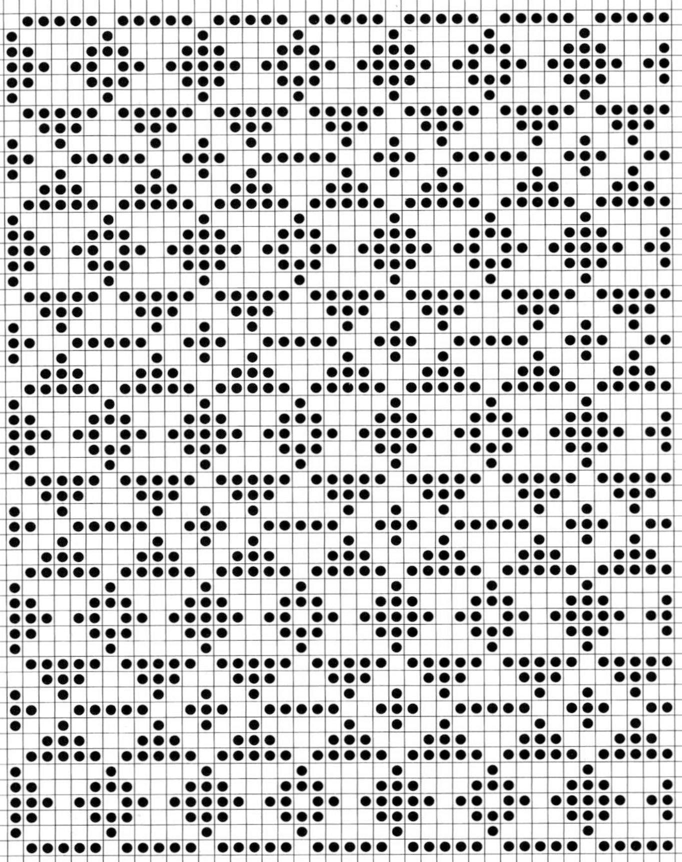

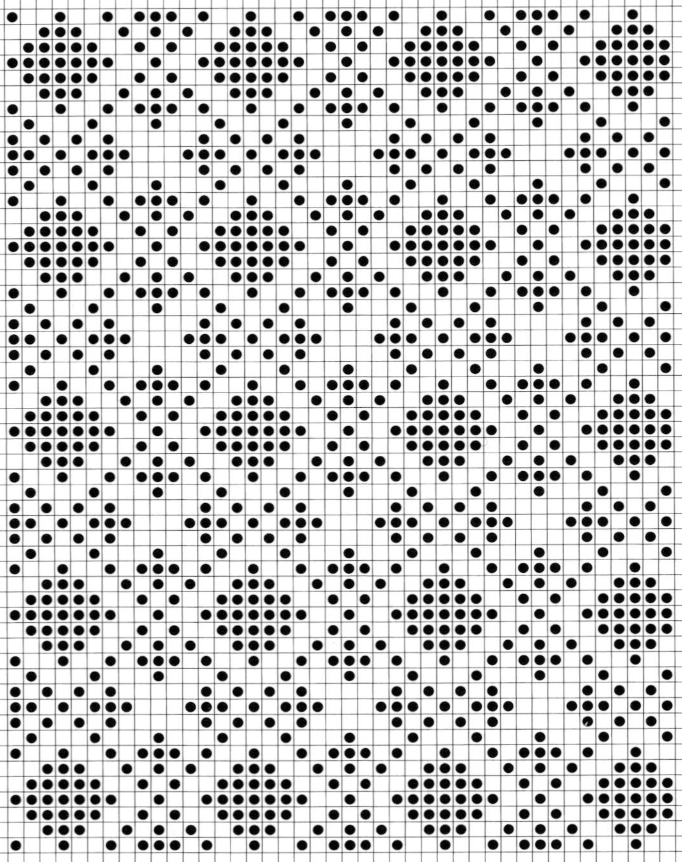

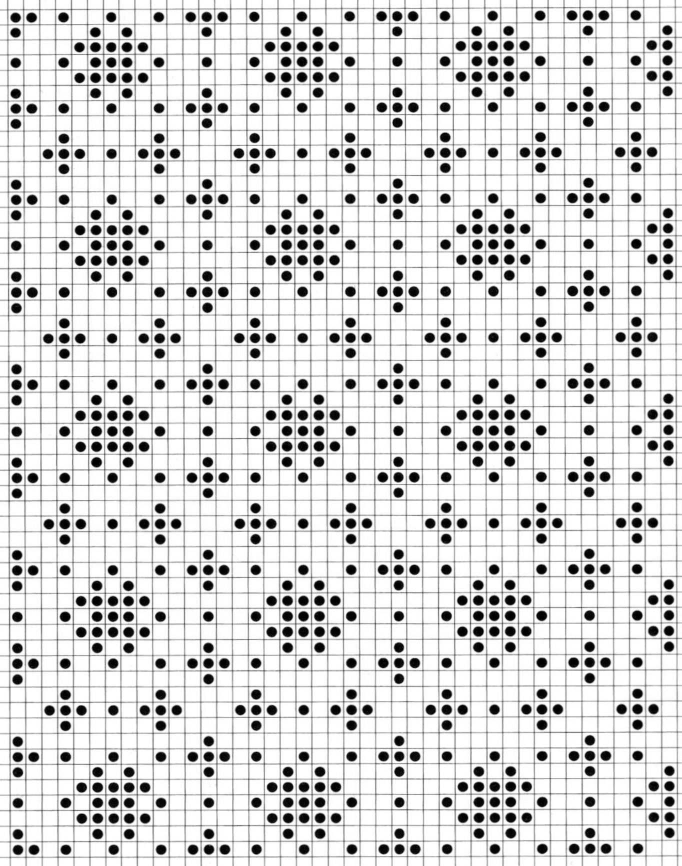

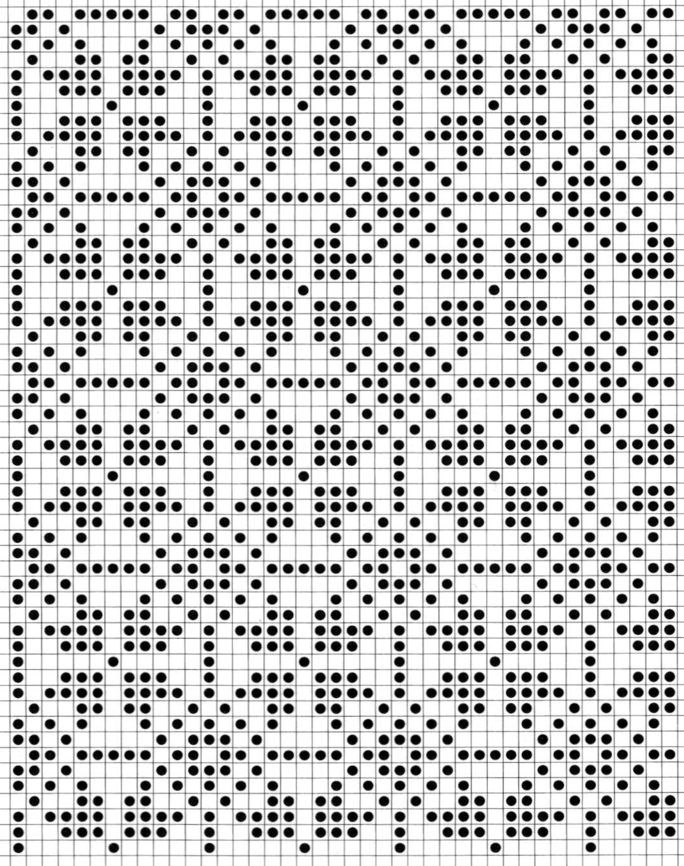

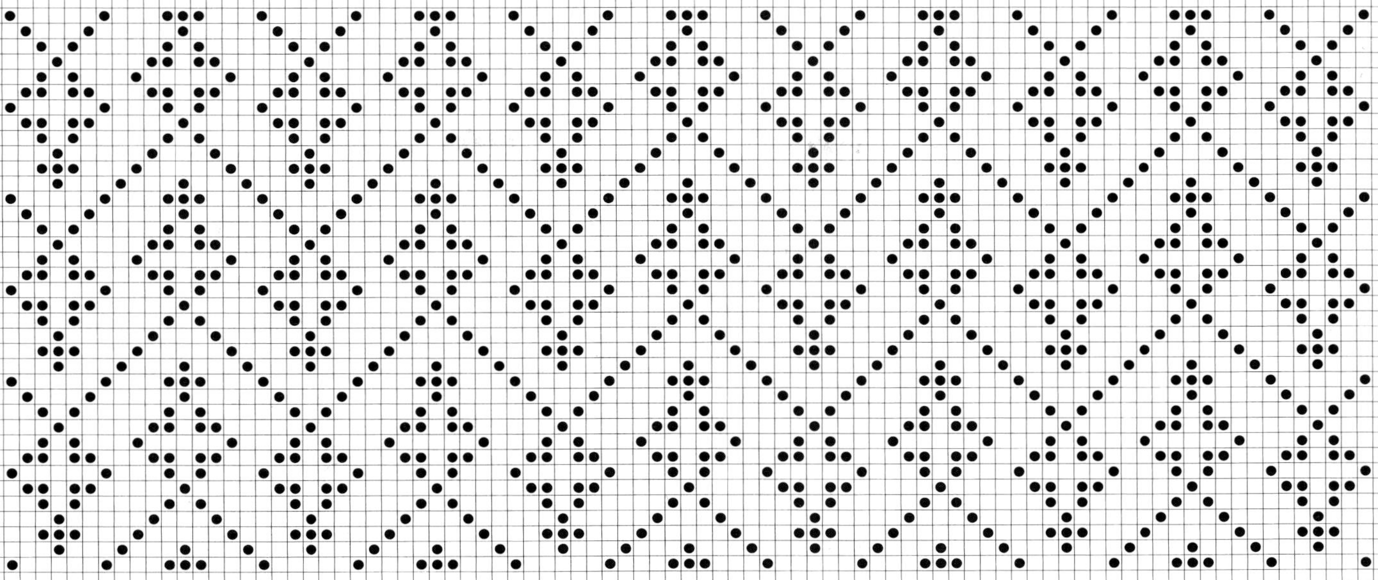

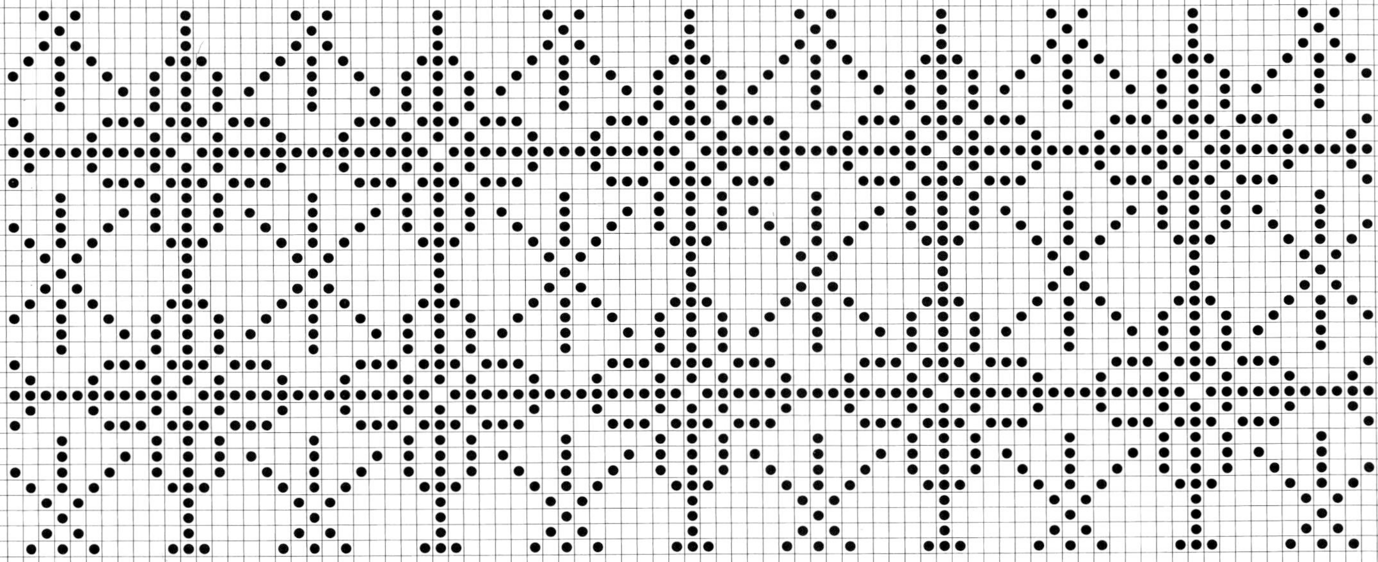

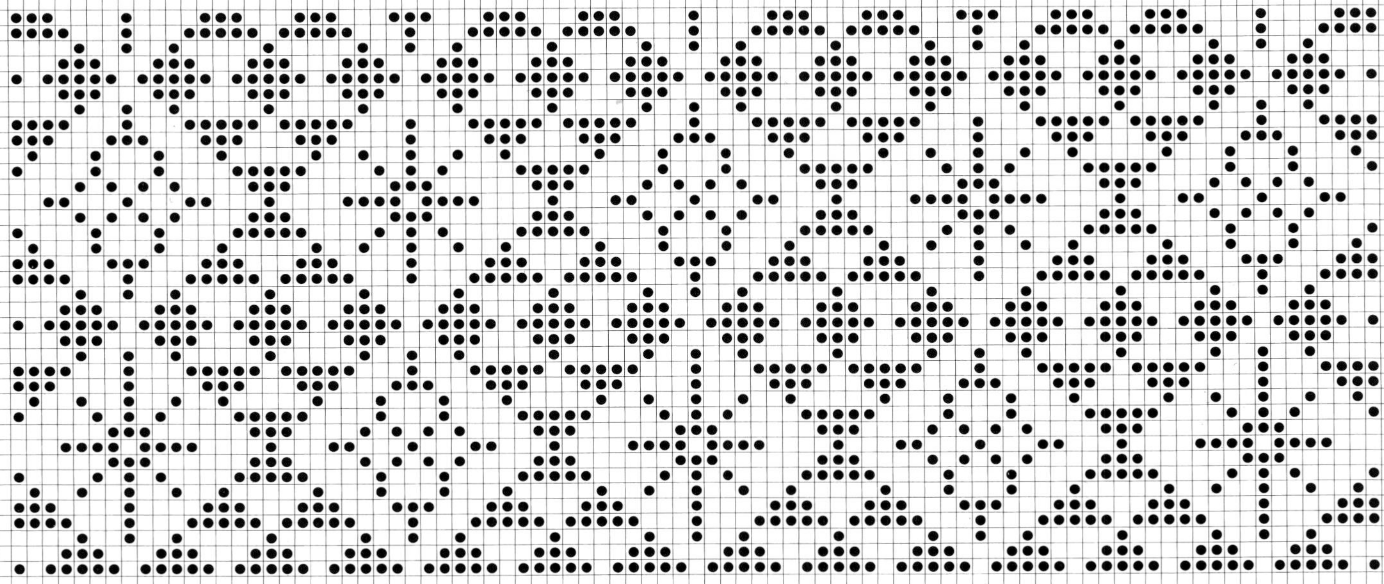

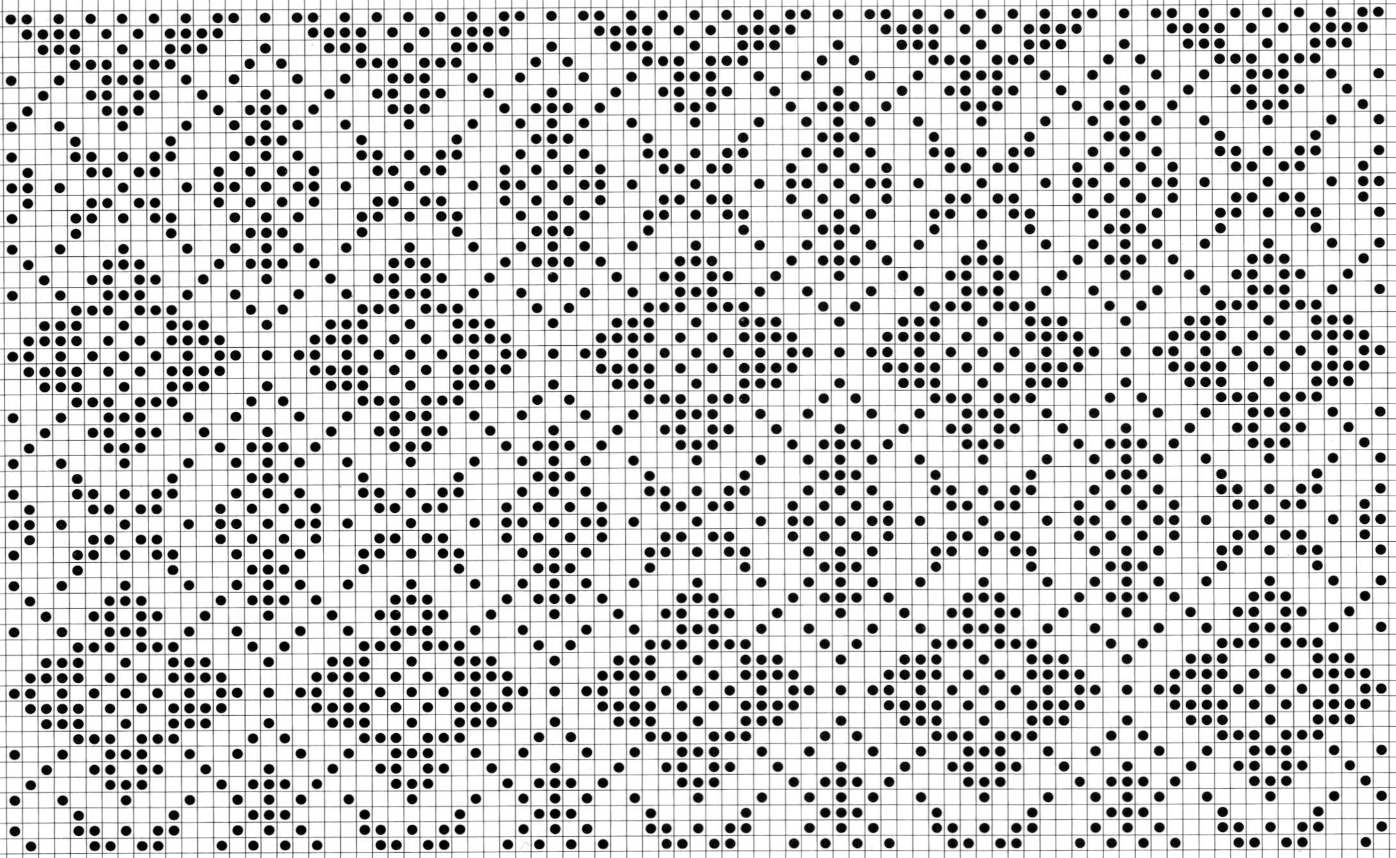

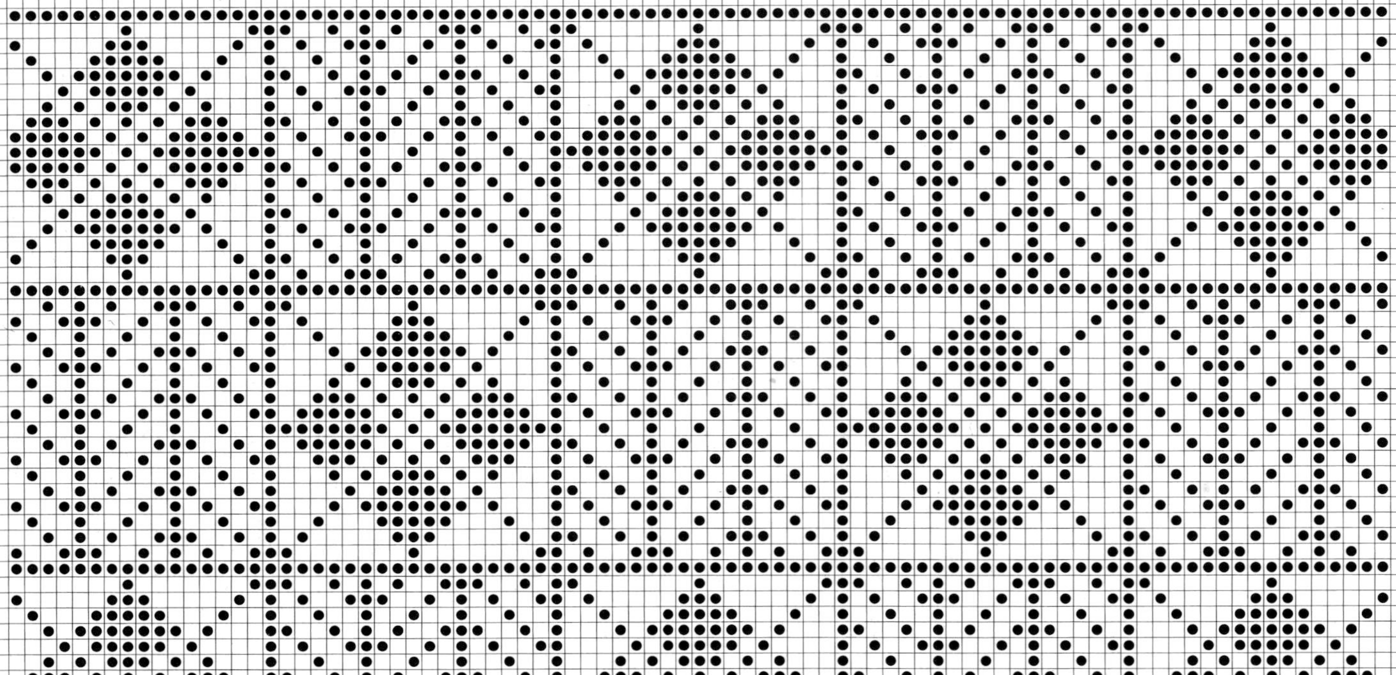

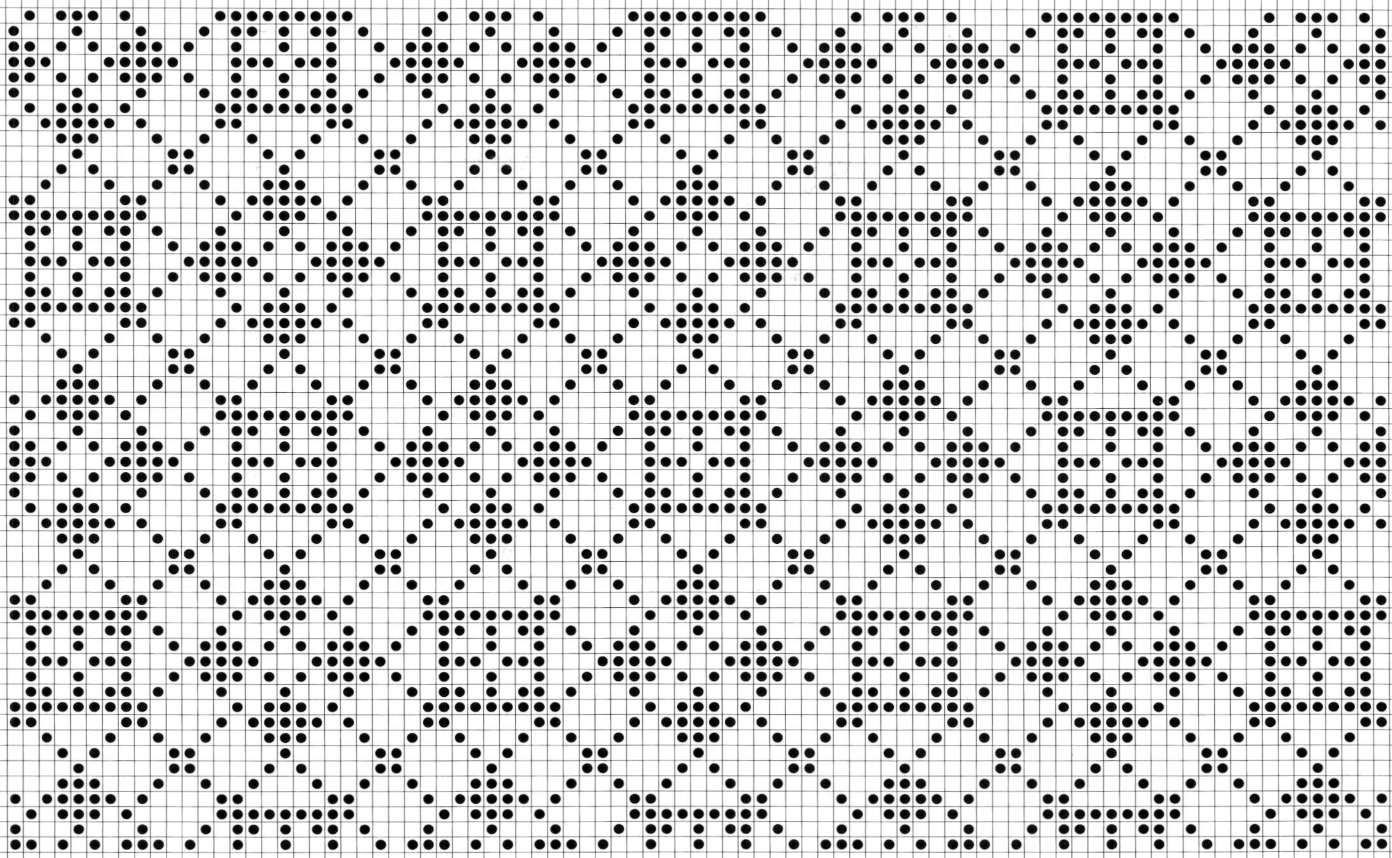

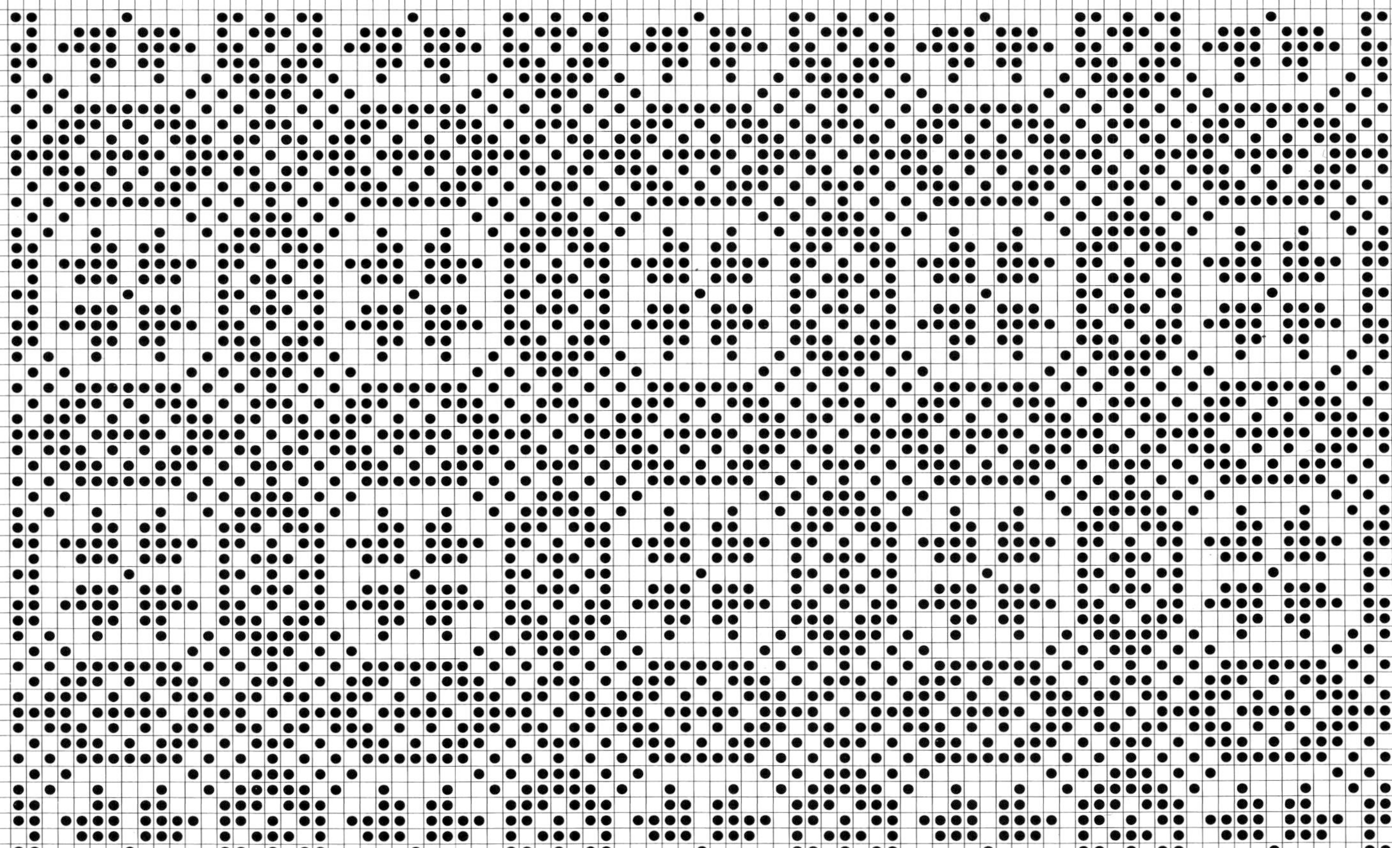

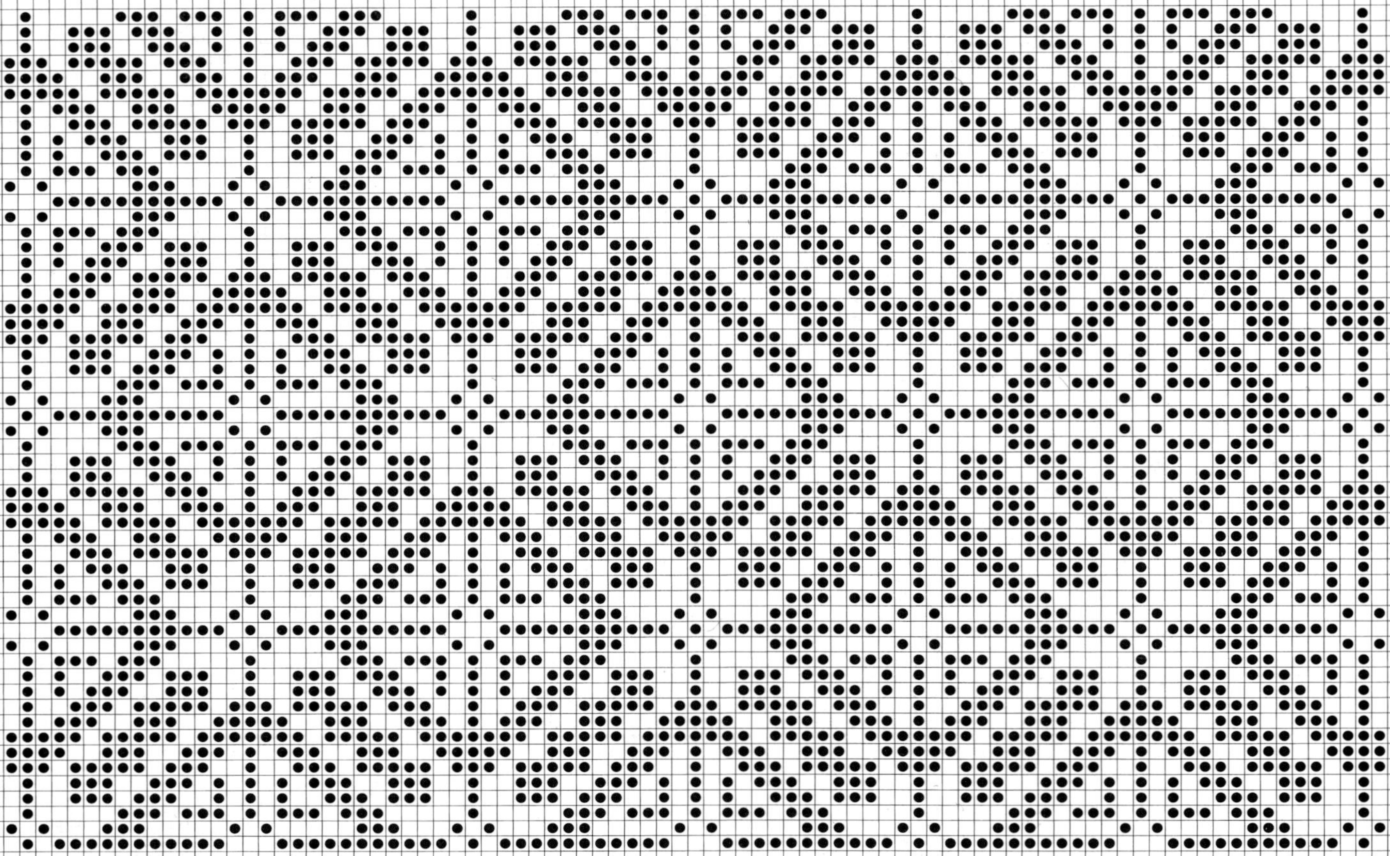

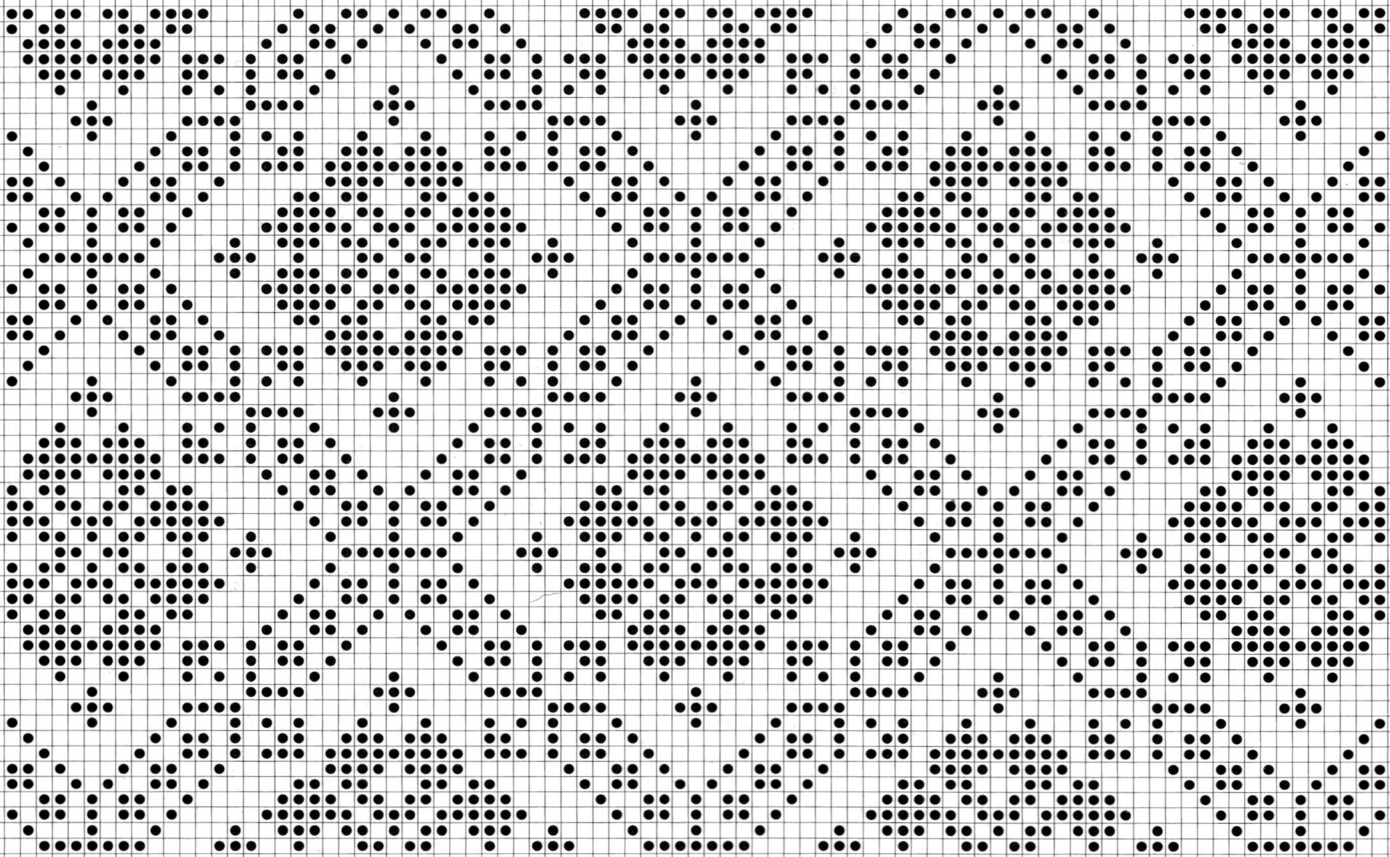

A Word on Colour

When compiling and writing this book in 1991, my intention was to provide knitters with a comprehensive pattern source. I hoped they would use it to create their own colour schemes and then go on to incorporate them into garments to suit themselves in both style and size. My aim was for a "desert island book"—the sole book a knitter would need if marooned somewhere with a set of needles and vast supply of yarn.

For that reason, I did not include any indications or prescriptions on the use of colour, and I kept the chapter on designing sweaters as simple as possible, covering the main points on how to work out size, and how to place patterns correctly within basic shapes. I felt this approach would give the widest scope for individual creativity, and judging from the initial response it seemed to work. I received very positive thanks not just from knitters, but from weavers, embroiderers—and even one cake decorator—who found the book useful and inspiring.

However, over the intervening years, many knitters have expressed to me a profound fear of working with colour, and, in many cases, a belief that they have "no eye" for it. This prevents them from even beginning to attempt colour schemes of their own, despite having this readily available source of patterns.

There is no formula I can give which will turn anyone into a successful colourist. If you use a formula then your results will be formulaic and will lack that magic sparkle that is the hallmark of a great design. The art has to come from your own mind and the eye must be your own, and it is here that you can make a start. I believe that everyone has the capacity to create work that will please them if they give themselves a chance. It does involve time and effort, and success may not come in an instant. It is vital to become excited about your project and to realise that the swatch you regard as a failure is actually a worthwhile experiment which you can study and learn from; this is an essential part of the creative process.

My instinct is to simply and briefly say: marvel with passion at the endless beauty in the world; surround yourself with beautiful yarns and colours and just plunge in. Essentially, that is how I work myself, but in order to explain further I invite you once again to "look over my shoulder" while I describe my thought processes in relation to some examples of my colour schemes.

Like any artist, I work with the best materials that I can lay my hands on. Not only does this assure that the finished work will be as good as it can possibly be, it also provides inspiration and pleasure in itself, and makes the whole experience easier and more exciting. I am fortunate enough to be able to design my own yarns and colours, and I have created my Hebridean range of colours from pure wool, dyed in many shades in the fleece and then mixed into subtle blends which are then spun into yarn. This means that the colours play off one another when they are knitted or stitched in patterns, and a huge variety of effects can be achieved depending on which colours are juxtaposed and how much of each colour is used in the pattern. There is an alchemy that occurs that is always exciting to witness, and this adds to the pleasure of the process—and I consider enjoyment to be a very important factor in the creation of a successful design.

It is perfectly possible to create beautiful designs with a very simple colour scheme. If you want to start cautiously you can make a wrap, throw, or cushion cover by choosing a pattern and working in just two colours throughout. The patterns themselves can be enough to inspire ideas. Shown at left is an example of a Norwegian allover pattern from page 36. I liked the spacious floral, delicacy of the pattern arrangement within the simple diagonal geometry, and to keep that as the focus I knitted it in Hebridean 3 Ply in a Sea Ivory background, with the patterns worked in Lapwing. There is depth and interest in the blended colours, with the Sea Ivory providing a soft and warm effect while the glowing glints in the Lapwing emphasise the delicacy of the pattern. It is worth noting that solid dyed colours will produce a very different effect and will appear flat and harsh by comparison.

Now consider the Norwegian panels shown at right. For this example, I stayed with just two colours and allowed the patterns to dictate the direction. I chose horizontal borders from the Norwegian patterns on pages 26, 28 and 30 and an allover pattern from page 41. I like the bold geometry and the stylised half-flower imagery. Combining the horizontals with the vertical lines of the allover emphasises the geometry further, as does working the background and pattern colours of the largest horizontal band in opposition to the main vertical pattern. Hebridean 3 Ply in Selkie and Pebble Beach are the perfect foil for this arrangement: full of subtle interest in themselves, but sufficiently neutral to allow the graphic quality of the patterns to sing.

The two swatches shown above are examples of how you can take a little step along from working with just two colours of yarn throughout. I chose two of my own allover pattern designs from *The Inner Landscape* and worked them in Hebridean 2 Ply to make a pair of cushions for a particular decor. The unifying theme is the background colour of Golden Plover which remains the same throughout each pattern.

For the *Inner Landscape Diamond* (above left) I shaded the first pattern in Calluna,

Lapwing and Bog Bean in tune with the symmetry of the pattern, moving from the darkest, through the mid, to the lighter tone, so that the eye is directed to the centre of each diamond shape.

For the *Inner Landscape Lozenge* (above right) I changed the three blue shades—Mara, Shearwater and Witchflower—randomly to emphasise the twist and turn of the lozenges.

Generally speaking, when a pattern is symmetrical I use the symmetry to place the colours. It is an obvious marriage of the two

elements and gives cohesion to the whole scheme. It means that you can add in lots of colours and yet maintain the sense and flow of the pattern.

I designed this little *Floral Allover Pattern* (shown above) to represent a machair meadow on the Atlantic shoreline which was dominated by harebells, dandelions, lady's bedstraw and eyebright. I created stylised versions of the little petal shapes for the motifs in the pattern and I originally knitted it in the colours of the meadow, with a green background and flowers in blue, yellow and pale neutrals. This was a fairly close depiction of the scene, which is shown in a photograph on page 77 of my book of Fair Isle knitting. However, the pattern lends itself just as well to the myriad tiny plants and flowers of the moorland, so I have re-coloured it in the moorland version shown above, using six background and six pattern colours of Hebridean 2 Ply within the twenty pattern rows. I've graded the colours, one at a time, from the centre of one of the little flower motifs to the centre of the next. This is as many colours as I would use within this size of pattern as it can be overdone and the pattern can become lost when the eye has too much to cope with. It is also worth noting that when you are making a swatch, you should always place it at a distance to view the effect accurately. Try it with this photograph. Move a distance away from the book and you will see the pattern as it would appear in a design.

I find inspiration for pattern and colour everywhere, but especially in the landscape and seascape of the Outer Hebrides where I was born. I learned to dye colours from plants and lichens just as generations had done before me, so my relationship with colour in fleece and yarn began very early on. The sea and shoreline are a matter of yards from my door and every walk brings forth a bounty of ideas for pattern, colour and form.

The stitched piece, *Machair Shells* (above) is one small example. Machair is formed when calciferous shell sand blows onto acid moorland. Carefully managed grazing with cattle then ensures that this rare soil sustains a heavenly mix of plants and flowers which burst into bloom through summer.

The scallop shell and flower pattern shown above is one of my stylised interpretations of the machair. I dyed the yarns using plants and lichens from the moor and shoreline. It illustrates how even a small piece of work can contain a wealth of connections and personal experiences.

Exploring the shell theme further, winged symmetrical shapes of thin, delicate tellin shells were the basis for an allover pattern which I named *Luskentyre* (shown at right) after one of the great Atlantic beaches on which they can be found in huge numbers. I looked to their beautiful striped shades, ranging from pale ethereal tones to rich golds and deep purples, and worked the scheme in Hebridean 2 Ply.

Sometimes I use photography as a guide for colour schemes. I took the picture I call *Glass Wave* (above) at the foot of my croft one stormy day.

The wave was huge and powerful but for an instant it was caught in a shaft of light and turned into a green glass sculpture. It is astonishing to find delicate shells intact after such huge waves and storms have carried them ashore and I am always reminded that each one I pick up has had a precarious journey before it rests in my hand. This made me think of shells, waves and motion; I consequently came up with the *Wave Shell Pattern* (shown at right) and blended in the Glass Wave colours.

The natural world contains more inspiration than anyone could wish for in a lifetime and I am always keen to explore my surroundings no matter where I am. Designing from memories of places I have visited is an irresistible urge. I designed *Oregon* (shown at right) after a drive through that very beautiful state. I drove for many miles through huge forests of mainly coniferous trees. It was Spring and the deciduous tree buds showed up as a delicate sprinkle against the dark conifers. The Mackenzie River ran parallel to the road and new flowers and leaves made a colourful band in the undergrowth along its banks. I interpreted this with a tree motif strategically set in an allover pattern. I then created a horizontal leaf pattern to depict the river bank. I originally worked the design in remembrance of the colours I saw on that Spring day, emphasising the horizontal border by adding a few shades that are not in the main pattern. I saw Oregon again in the Autumn but I had to wait to create my Hebridean yarn palette before I was able to capture the effect in the Autumn version, shown here.

Just as with the pattern, colour ideas can also be triggered from many other sources. For example, *Grant Avenue* (above and at right) came into being as a result of a visit to San Francisco's Chinatown area. I found it exotic, thronging with life and brim full of colourful artefacts.

Among the many delights that caught my eye were lovely lacquer-work pieces. I took home many memories of glowing colours and eastern pattern styles, and played around with these to create the patterns for this design. I wanted to draw particular attention to the border so I picked it out in reds and brighter blues, while working the smaller-scale allover pattern in golds and shades of darker blues and greens.

Most of the patterns in this book are highly suited to the stranded knitting technique which is best worked using just two colours in each row. As you can see from the examples I have shown, you can create very colourful effects in this way, by changing the colours at intervals throughout the pattern. You can also add more colour to a two colour pattern by Swiss darning (duplicate stitching) colours on top. This is preferable to carrying more than two colours along the rows which will result in too much bulk in the knitted piece. Here, I have knitted the butterfly pattern on page 113 in just two colours of Hebridean 2 Ply and then Swiss darned little spots of colour on to the motif. This can be done discreetly or to any extent that you desire.

There are innumerable sources of inspiration out there for each of us to find and interpret in our own personal way. My hope is that you will find this book of some assistance—perhaps a jumping-off point—be you knitter, stitcher, weaver, cake decorator, or anyone who just wants to explore working with patterns.

For those of you who by now are hooked on pattern, the end of this book is just a temporary stop. The next ports of call will be determined by what you see, and, most importantly, where your imagination leads you. Wherever that is and wherever it takes you—*bon voyage*.

Alice Starmore® Yarns

are available exclusively from

www.virtualyarns.com

an online yarn shop supplying knitters throughout the world.

Free air mail delivery on all sweater kits.

All swatches and garments photographed in this book are made with **Alice Starmore®** *Hebridean 2 & 3 Ply* yarns, with the exception of—

• the swatches on the *Introduction* page and page 142, which are made with natural-dyed wool yarn.

• the swatches on pages 78 and 79, which are made with **Alice Starmore®** *Hebridean 2 Ply* and hand-dyed silk yarn.

The hand-knitted garments photographed in this book are— *Grant Avenue*, *Marina* cardigan and *Oregon* cardigan, Autumn version. They are available as kits, with full instructions and yarns, from

www.virtualyarns.com

with thanks

For invaluable assistance while researching the traditional knitting chapter in this book

The Swedish Institute, Stockholm

Nordiska Museet, Stockholm

Norsk Folkemuseum, Oslo

Ministry of Foreign Affairs, Helsinki

National Museum, Helsinki

The Winston Churchill Memorial Trust

Model, Tara

Model, Bogusia
Make-up Artist, Taiyyibah Bashir

Model, Numba
Make-up Artist, Taiyyibah Bashir

Swatch photography,
fashion photography & styling

Jade Starmore

Model, Sophia
Make-up Artist, Sarah Foggarty

ABOUT THE AUTHOR

Alice Starmore is a Scottish artist, photographer, designer, and author whose textile books are in use throughout the world. She was born on the Hebridean island of Lewis into a typical family of Gaelic speaking crofter-fishermen. The culture in which she was brought up and the nature of the landscape around her have greatly influenced her work.

She became a professional textile designer in 1975 and three years later was awarded a Winston Churchill Fellowship which enabled her to travel to Norway, Sweden, and Finland to study the textile traditions of those countries. She started to write after this, and has since had sixteen books published, plus numerous magazine articles. She has established an international reputation as a leading expert on knitting design and technique. This book on Fair Isle knitting and her book *Aran Knitting* are regarded as important standard texts on their subjects, and she has taught and lectured extensively throughout Britain, Europe, and the USA.

In 2001, along with her daughter Jade, she created her unique range of Alice Starmore® Hebridean Yarn for Virtual Yarns Ltd., their on-line yarn and design company which showcases and sells their classic and current knitting design work.

Photography, drawing, and painting are constant threads weaving through all aspects of her career. Her current work in these media tends strongly towards the natural world and is often linked to nature conservancy. She is an authority on the flora and fauna of Hebridean moorlands habitats.

For more of her work see:

www.alicestarmore.com (photography and the natural world)
www.mamba.org.uk (gallery exhibitions)
www.virtualyarns.com (knitting and textiles)

Published Books

1. *Scandinavian Knitwear*, 1981, Bell & Hyman, UK.
2. *Knitting From the British Islands*, 1982, Bell & Hyman, UK; St. Martin's Press, USA.
3. *Children's Knitting From Many Lands*, 1983, Bell & Hyman, UK.
4. *Alice Starmore's Book of Fair Isle Knitting*, 1988, Tauton Press, USA.
   also published as *The Fair Isle Knitting Handbook* by Blandford Book, UK.
   Published in 2009 by Dover Publications Inc., USA.
5. *Sweaters for Men*, 1988, Ballantine Books, USA; Pavilion Books, UK.
6. *The Celtic Collection*, 1992, Anaya, UK; Trafalgar Square, USA.
7. *Charts for Colour Knitting*, 1992, Windfall Press, UK.
8. *Fishermen's Sweaters*, 1993, Anaya UK; Trafalgar Square, USA; also translated into Swedish and published as *Fiskartröjor*, 1995, Raben-Prisma, Sweden.
9. *Celtic Needlepoint*, 1994, Anaya UK; Trafalgar Square, USA.
10. *In the Hebrides*, 1995, Windfall Press for The Broad Bay Company, USA.
11. *Stillwater*, 1996, Windfall Press for The Broad Bay Company, USA.
12. *Aran Knitting*, 1997, Interweave Press, USA. Expanded Edition published in 2010 by Dover Publications Inc., USA.
13. *Pacific Coast Highway*, 1997, Windfall Press for The Broad Bay Company, USA.
14. *Tudor Roses*, 1998, Windfall Press for The Broad Bay Company, USA.
15. *The Children's Collection* (with Jade Starmore), 2000, Interweave Press, USA.
16. *Road Movies Volume 1*, 2008, Windfall Press, UK.

Also several articles for *Threads* magazine, USA.
Designs, articles, and video on Fair Isle Knitting for *Vogue Knitting* magazine, USA.
Articles and photographs for *Dragonfly News*, UK.

Published Papers

"Submerged oviposition behaviour in the Large Red Damselfly *Pyrrhosoma nymphula* (Sulzer) on the Isle of Lewis."
"Journal of the British Dragonfly Society," UK, Volume 24, No. 2, 2008.

Major Exhibitions

Mamba, first shown at An Lanntair Gallery, Stornoway, UK, 2008.

Sources of Supply

Alice Starmore designed her range of 2 Ply Hebridean luxury pure wool yarn in 2000 as the ideal medium for designs using the Fair Isle techniques explained in this book. Alice Starmore® Hebridean yarns and a comprehensive range of current designs using these methods are available globally and can be ordered directly from www.virtualyarns.com